# Four Decades in The Dental Profession

*A Personal Memoir*

# Adejoke A. Fatunde, BDS, MS, Sc.D.

To order additional copies of this book, contact:
Xlibris
844-714-8691
www.Xlibris.com
Orders@Xlibris.com

ISBN: 978-1-6641-7182-4 (sc)
ISBN: 978-1-6641-7183-1 (hc)
ISBN: 978-1-6641-7181-7 (e)

Library of Congress Control Number: 2021908618

Print information available on the last page.

Rev. date: 08/29/2022

From the blessings and lessons of the past
I am enjoying the gift of the present

and…

I am motivated by
What my future may hold
and
How those after me will do greater things.

While I can,
I plan to make the best of each moment
for as long as
I have the breadth
and
strength of God in me.


Adejoke Ariyike Fatunde
(2021)

# CONTENTS

**01** CHAPTER I:
**INTRODUCTION**

**11** CHAPTER II:
**UNIVERSITY EDUCATION - CASTING THE VOTE FOR DENTISTRY**

**13** CHAPTER III:
**THE SOJOURN THROUGH THE UNIVERSITY OF IBADAN DENTAL SCHOOL: 1975 -1980**

**17** CHAPTER IV:
**BEYOND THE UNIVERSITY OF IBADAN DENTAL SCHOOL**

**59** CHAPTER V:
**RECONNECTING WITH THE UI PIONEER DENTAL CLASS AFTER 40 YEARS SINCE GRADUATION FROM DENTAL SCHOOL**

**65** CHAPTER VI:
**GRATITUDE**

**67** CHAPTER VII:
**WORDS FROM THE POTTERS**

**75** CHAPTER VIII:
**FROM THE SUPERVISORS**

**79** CHAPTER IX:
**FRIENDS UNFORGETTABLE**

**83** CHAPTER X:
**MY MOTIVATORS AND DESTINY HELPERS**

**87** CHAPTER XI:
**CONCLUSION**

CHAPTER I:

# INTRODUCTION

<u>Pre-Dental: Early Life & Elementary Education</u>

I was born in Ede, now located in Oshun State, Nigeria to Adebowale and Omoyisola (nee Adeyi) Atanda and given the names, Adejoke Ariyike Ayinke Atanda. I am the first of six children of these two parents. I am married to Dr. Ayodeji Fatunde, and we are blessed with four children.

Both of my parents were teachers by profession. Talk of two people who had a desire to be the best and were focused on their goals, no matter in which aspect of life, it was these two who gave me life. They worked in tandem to achieve the goals they mapped out individually, together as a couple and for their children.

They both started as Grade II teachers after their teacher training and taught in several elementary and secondary or high schools but had desire for higher education. While teaching, my dad undertook the required examinations for university admission. In the Fall of 1959, he enrolled at the University College London, Ibadan campus which later became the University of Ibadan (UI), Ibadan, Oyo State, Nigeria for his Bachelor of Arts degree in History. While dad was in Ibadan, my mom, my immediate brother, Dewale and I remained in Ikire, now in Oshun State, Nigeria, about two hours away by road. Mom continued with her teaching job as she nurtured us.

Two years into my dad's university program, my maternal grandmother passed away, leaving a heartbroken grandpa. Worried about the depth of his grief, my parents knew they could not leave him alone by himself in Lagos. Grandpa on the other hand, refused to move from the house he shared with grandma, the repertoire of his memories of her. All efforts to persuade him to move from Lagos and live with us in Ikire proved abortive. My parents then decided that mom, along with us children, should move to Lagos and live with grandpa. Our company was expected to have two advantages. First, my parents hoped that our living with grandpa will provide him company and that engaging in our care would be activities that will take up part of the time spent grieving for his darling wife. Secondly, they envisaged that living in the same house with us would help him and his only daughter (my mom) and youngest of their three children grieve together and heal together, sooner than later from the pain of their loss.

Thus, just in time for the start of the equivalent of first grade, we moved to Lagos which was a different environment. In contrast to me, it was homecoming for mom as she knew almost everyone in her old neighborhood. She navigated every corner of 90 Tokunbo Street in Lagos, Nigeria with ease and familiarity. We attended First Baptist Church on Broad Street, Lagos, the same church where she worshipped every Sunday while she was home and where she got married. In no time, she caught up with her old friends and their children became my cohort of friends who welcomed me very warmly. I was assimilated into the church groups in a similar way.

Mom enrolled me in the Brownie Group that met at a location near my school. On Wednesdays, I would quickly change to Brownie uniform after school, head down the road for meetings and walk back to our church at First Baptist Church to meet mom for the midweek service before going home. She also registered me for Girl's Brigade and my unit met at the African Church Cathedral, Bethel on the same street as our church. Brigade meetings took place on Sundays after church. My white uniform always accompanied me to church, ready to be donned after church service. These activities helped me expand my network of friends, kept me engaged in addition to school and almost made me oblivious to the change of moving from small town Ikire to Lagos, the capital city.

School, however, was a different story. I enrolled at a new school, Ade-Oshodi Memorial Baptist School on St. Savior Street in Lagos. This was the same school my mom attended for elementary education. My luck drew me into the class of Mrs. Ola, who was my mother's first grade teacher. I either did not smile like my mom, or my writing was not as neat as my mother's. No matter how much I minded myself, my mom remained with me in Mrs. Ola's classroom even though she taught in a different school at the opposite end of town. Except for interactions with Riyike, whom I knew from church and whose first name was the same as my middle name, I kept pretty much to myself. The fear of doing something that might seem wrong to Mrs. Ola enhanced my reserved nature.

My grandpa did the school run on foot; walked my brother and I to school and picked us up every day. Our daily commute became my venting sessions. He encouraged me to see Mrs. Ola's comments from a positive perspective and assured me that what she wanted was to make me uphold high standards and that was for my good. Grandpa provided the emotional cushion I needed as we walked home from school each day. He was never in a hurry, listening to me talk about the different events of the day. If I was confused about something, he immediately addressed it, illustrating his explanations many times with written communication, usually in a timely manner. If he deemed the issue urgent enough, he would address it before we got home. This he did sometimes using the sand serving as his blackboard and any piece of stick he found nearby as the chalk.

Once we got home, the first order of business was finishing my homework. Then, it was time to tackle mom's assignments that were often more rigorous than the ones given in class. On one hand, it was helpful in that I could breeze through class work but, I could not be seen to be doing nothing thereafter. That only got me in more trouble with Mrs. Ola who would find additional exercises for me for sitting 'idle' in class while others were busy doing their class work. I was more than glad to be done with Mrs. Ola's first grade and looked forward to second grade being relatively uneventful for me. However, my immediate brother, Dewale also got Mrs. Ola as his first-grade teacher. That did not sit well with me, and I considered it unfair.

I pondered on the probability that a mother and her two children would have the same first grade teacher across decades. Did Mrs. Ola request for my brother, even if my placement was by chance or could the placement for both of us have been a coincidence? Not that I could reverse the placements, but my young mind could not help but reflect on this every time I got called to Mrs. Ola's class to learn of my brother's latest escapades for onward transmission to mom.

The day I heard her tell my brother 'I taught your mother and your sister, and each of them was a delight in my class', I could not believe my ears! I was ecstatic, to my brother's chagrin as I reported this to grandpa on the way home. Grandpa let me know he had a chat with Mrs. Ola as soon as I expressed my feelings. He said that Mrs. Ola did not give him any bad reports about me. He reiterated his earlier message that whatever she told me was only to bind me to a high standard and assured my brother of the same message. My experience with a generational teacher such as Mrs. Ola was impactful. It kept me on my toes and left me little room for mistakes. It taught me to digest and accept criticisms when valid and take negativity as challenges to make better decisions. I also learnt to take definite actions to address unpleasant reports even when it appears unfair, unwarranted, or unjustified.

My dad completed his first degree and immediately enrolled for a doctoral degree at the University of Ibadan. When he was about finishing his Ph.D. program, dad came to interview for a Lecturer position to teach History at the University of Lagos (Unilag) in Lagos, the same city where we lived with grandpa. My mom and I accompanied dad and we toured the Unilag campus while he interviewed. We visited the University Staff School where I would be attending, and I was excited about living and attending school on Unilag campus. My excitement fuelled my fascination with the new school, and I had dreams about the activities I would engage in once I started school there.

My dreams however proved short-lived after my parents informed me that we were moving to the University of Ibadan campus not, the University of Lagos. Initially, this news left me dumbfounded for days. I wondered how I would cope without the emotional support that grandpa provided. I was mindful of the fact that we moved to Lagos because grandpa remained immovable from the house that held his memories of grandma. Finally, after many days, I shared my anxiety about leaving grandpa by himself and losing the emotional support he provided for me with my parents. They were empathic, but the decision was settled. Neither their words of assurance nor their hugs gave me any comfort at that moment.

I half-hoped that grandpa would change his mind and decide to move with us. At the time of the proposed move, there were two more children in addition to Dewale and me. Deleye was five years old and Deboye, three years old. We had lived with grandpa almost five years and all four of his grandchildren from my mom were closely attached to him. However, I was not surprised to know that option was not available. Grandpa still would not leave his repertoire of memories. Instead, he supported my parents' decision and urged them to pursue their desired future. He showed immense appreciation for their sacrifice of almost five years that my family lived with him to help him overcome his grief. He assured them he will be all right by himself and promised me he would visit often.

Off we were to another city, another school, and an unfamiliar environment in a city that was almost a two-hour drive away from grandpa. I was scared as I had no idea what to expect now that it would be a new experience not only for me but, for mom too. She had the last move back to her home environment under her belt. On the contrary, this new move was a new life for all of us, mom included. It was a move that I did not look forward to by any means.

We arrived in Ibadan in time for me to start the equivalent of fifth grade at the University of Ibadan Staff School and changed to Abadina School after the first semester. Both schools were located on the campus of the University of Ibadan and a relatively short commute from our house on Lander Road on the same campus. Grandpa remained true to his word, unfailingly appeared the day before each trimester ended and would make sure he visited my teacher. He also came for field day and other events at school. I was able to share my fears and anxieties with him. He always listened and counseled me, reminding me that preparations helped him succeed and that I should follow in his footsteps. He remained my pillar of support.

Now that dad was settled into his job as a Lecturer in History at the University of Ibadan, it was mom's turn to acquire higher education. She went back to school while she continued to work as a teacher, nurture and watch her children grow. She did not stop until she got her Bachelor of Arts degree (B.A.) in History. Neither did her additional home schooling for each of us children ever take a break. Most of the household chores were primarily mine to execute. In addition, it was my responsibility to ensure my brothers performed their chores, or else, I would take the heat. I had no room for boredom and no chance to get slack in getting my duties completed. Each task I failed to complete invited trouble from mom. Multitasking became my coping skill and my escape from trouble was to embrace focus. In hindsight, she was preparing me for life even though at the time, I was convinced that I had the strictest mother on earth.

## Pre-Dental: High School or Secondary School Education

For secondary school or high school, I attended Queen's School in Ibadan, Nigeria and was in the boarding house. There, I had very notable seven years preparing for both the ordinary (O/L) and advanced level (A/L) general certificate examinations (GCE) that were pre-requisites for university education. At Queen's School, I learnt to organize and prioritize. In addition to didactics, many skills were taught that have remained with me for a lifetime.

The extracurricular activities offered were robust and I got involved in quite a few; choir, debate, track, netball, drama and French Club. There, I grew into Girl's Guide as an advancement from the Brownie experience I had in Lagos. Knowing that it was a case of no pass, no play, my focus had to be academics and the multi-tasking I had learnt to embrace gave me the flexibility to enjoy these activities. A hallmark of our education at Queen's School was confidence building taught by all the teachers, house mistresses and the principals.

My second year in Queen's School equipped me to learn self-reliance. My dad elected to go on a one-year sabbatical leave to the University of Chicago in Chicago, Illinois in the United States of America (USA) and the whole family except me went with him. My parents decided that my education at Queen's School was not to be disturbed for the one year in Chicago and expressed the same to me. That is how pristine they held Queen's School.

I spent most of that year at school, learnt to take care of myself and make decisions on many issues that required quick answers and for which I did not have the luxury of seeking guidance or approval from my parents. Mom and dad were across the ocean, letters took two weeks one way at the earliest and many decisions could not wait till I wrote to Chicago and got a response back. I learnt to arrive at my decisions in a stepwise manner, making sure I had a reason for eliminating or adding each step so I could explain the rationale behind my choice to mom and dad. Unknowingly, I was learning the art of deductive reasoning.

My highlight of the week were the letters I received from mom and dad and while that was not a substitute for their physical presence, I was kept in the loop about family events. I enjoyed journaling in my two-column notebook that mom handed me the day they left for Chicago. She had me journal my experiences every week of the one year in one column while the other column featured the lessons I learnt from each event. That kept me accountable as I knew I would be grilled by mom on the pros and cons of each of my decisions. That exercise gave me appreciation both for what I had and what I wished I had, what I learned to do and what I needed to work on to improve.

During vacations from school, I was in the care of Mr. and Mrs. D.A. Ologunde of blessed memory. I remain grateful to them both and to their family. They were good friends with my parents and lived on the campus of University of Ibadan. However, they went beyond friendship to take loving care of me.

In Queen's school, I grew up with sisters, albeit non-biological sisters. With these sisters, I developed relationships that have lasted a lifetime. From each of them, I learnt the value of accommodation, the art of supporting one another, empathy, and sacrifice. These life-long friendships developed the humanity in me and ultimately influenced my academic and career achievements. I am appreciative of the fellowships I share with my classmates and the love that still binds our hearts together today with more than fifty years of memories. Attending the fiftieth-year reunion with my classmates from Queen's School in October-November 2019 brought alive many of these unforgettable memories that remain a great treasure.

Queen's School, no doubt, was my preparatory school for tertiary education as well as for life. I am thankful to all the teachers at Queen's School, Ibadan, Nigeria who invested their time, energy, and guidance into me. I am grateful that my parents chose Queen's School amongst all the secondary schools to which I was admitted. This choice opened the golden gate to vibrant years and opportunities for me later in life.

Before I knew it, one year was over and my family was back together. Reuniting with my parents and siblings gave me a fresh awareness of the blessings of being in a family. I did not realize how much I had missed my three 'musketeer' brothers, Dewale, Deleye and Deboye. In the one year they were away, they all seemed to have grown up in many ways. On their return, there were less events of their 'gang up' against me or leaving their chores undone which always got me in trouble with mom. I certainly missed my no-nonsense little sister Denike, who even at her incredibly young age, could hold her own waters, no matter who she was dealing with. My youngest brother, Desola, was a 'bun in the oven' when the family returned from Chicago and, I had the privilege of taking care of him after he was born. He was too young to join the three musketeers in their plots or compete with their speed at the runs or at playing ball. Hence, his little self was content to hang out with us girls at the time.

Four years after they returned from Chicago, we lost Mom, Denike and Desola in an automobile accident, all on the same May Day. It was indeed a miracle that my dad, of the four of them in the car survived, with a lot of injuries, but he was alive. This threw me a cold blow for a while. I was simply angry that God would allow this to happen. I struggled with my faith and could not understand what people meant when they told me 'God knows best' or 'We'll understand by and by' or any of the cliché phrases uttered by sympathizers in moments of grief.

Nothing made sense at the time, and I simply moved like a zombie, unable to understand why I had to lose my mother and my youngest two siblings; my only sister who was six years old and youngest brother who was just three years old. Worse still, was the fact that I lost all three in one day! It did not seem real and for a long time, it felt I was simply having a bad dream and would wake up to see they were all still with us. Facing the reality that none of them was ever coming back had a a tremendous shattering that took only the grace of God to cope with. That this happened at a very vulnerable age, three weeks short of my sixteenth birthday made the rest of my teenage and young adult life more arduous than I imagined it would have been. Too many times. I wondered what I might have done differently if I could get mom's counselling on my career. Once I showed interest in dentistry, she immediately made preliminary inquiries about dentistry at the University of Lagos. She had talked often about how she and dad would pay me monthly visits in Lagos if I went there to study dentistry. She certainly would have kept me on my toes.

My parents built the foundation for my professional life through the discipline instilled in me. My grandpa always served as my pillar of emotional support at every level of my growth and education. Distance never kept him away in all the years from elementary school through high school. Even when I was in dental school, grandpa came frequently, checking to make sure that all was well with me. He was at my dental school graduation and was at my wedding. He got to hold and bless my first child and his impact in my life remains unforgettable.

I have been blessed with a loving family and reminisces of my beautiful childhood, my teenage and early adulthood years bring me a lot of joy. This, without a doubt, in addition to the foundational training I received from my parents and grandpa has been majorly contributory to everything I have been privileged to achieve.

I am grateful to all the teachers under whose tutelage I learnt and grew. They instilled in me, the desire to soar and excel. My special thanks to Mrs. Ola, my generational teacher as I call her, for continuously challenging me from an early age.

*With my siblings: left to right:*
*Front row: Adeleye. Adenike, Adesola and Adeboye*
*Back row: Adewale and myself*

*My three 'Musketeer' brothers: L-R: Adeleye, Adewale and Adeboye*

*Grandpa: Samuel Folorunso Adeyi*

*Dad and Mom: Professor Adebowale and Mrs. Omoyisola Atanda*

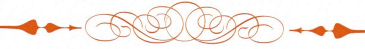

CHAPTER II:

# UNIVERSITY EDUCATION - CASTING THE VOTE FOR DENTISTRY

I always wanted to wear a white coat from as far back as I could remember. I enjoyed playing the doctor both at home and in plays at school. My role model then was Dr. Adenike Abiose who graduated from the University of Ibadan Medical School, and I had my mind set on studying medicine. That however began to change after we moved to Ibadan from Lagos.

After the move, my mom caught up with her friend's sister who was a dental hygienist. Mom periodically took us children to get dental cleaning at the Dugbe Dental Center in Ibadan. I was fascinated by the sound of the dentist's engine, the name I called the dental hand piece then. I asked the dentist lots of questions and simply marveled at the dental clinic each time I went there. The hygienist sometimes let me hold the water pipe, my appellation for suction tube while she cleaned my siblings' teeth. I remained quietly intrigued with the dental setting.

By the time I finished the equivalent of tenth grade or Form V and completed the Ordinary General Examination (O/levels) in 1973, I was no longer dogmatic about medicine. I became inquisitive about dentistry and learnt that the only dental school in Nigeria at the time was in Lagos. My parents reached out to their friends at the University of Lagos to make initial inquiries. Knowing grandpa still lived in Lagos, I was not against going to university in Lagos. My parents and I were settled with a tentative plan to go to Lagos if I still wanted to pursue dentistry.

However, my faith and resolve got tested with the death of my mom and youngest two siblings in 1974 when I was in the equivalent of eleventh grade. For that trimester, I changed from a border to a day student status at Queen's School. Leaving the boarding house where I only needed to deal with school meant that I was faced with juggling commuting to school by public transport for two hours one way, coping with school and homework, taking care of my siblings and other responsibilities at home. Despite my multi-tasking skills, I was overwhelmed but knew quitting was not an option.

My dad was immensely helpful in addressing my emotional challenges even though he was dealing with the loss of mom and my two youngest siblings with whom he co-habited the car at the time of the accident. He was also recovering from injuries sustained in the accident that claimed three lives from our family on the same day. He encouraged me not to bottle up my feelings and would engage me often to talk about mom and my siblings who passed away. He would constantly re-assure me that we would get through the pain even if we never understand why the loss of our family members happened. Those were dark days but, dad's strength held me up and gave me hope. Grandpa stood by us stoically with his faith in God. It was amazing that although he lost his only daughter and youngest of his three children, he focused all his energy on upholding those of us still able to breathe. He visited often, would take Dewale on trips, take time to talk to me and was always there, supporting us all.

My father always loved music. He served as the organist in church and sang duets with mom on many occasions. After the accident, he dug deeper into music and bought a piano. He would play for hours, some of the songs that he and mom loved, many of which I had heard them sing. By default, I sang along and soon found that music was a great healing therapy for me too. Slowly, the tears stopped flooding to a trickle, and I picked up my focus again.

Dad was not just a Professor of History; he was also my mathematics coach. Without his tutoring, I may not have passed Advanced Level Physics which was required for admission into most fields in the health sciences. After one of the tutoring sessions, I once asked him why he chose history, knowing how good he was in mathematics and physical sciences? His response was "You do your best and allow God to plant you where He wants you to be most fruitful for His glory". He was intriguingly versatile and able to discuss many disciplines with fervor.

When it was time to take the entrance examination for university admission, I could not leave family in Ibadan and scaled back on the desire to study dentistry since it was only available in Lagos. Dad encouraged me to apply to the University of Lagos if dentistry was my first choice but, I did not have the heart to leave Ibadan. About the same time, grandpa's landlady decided the house which was the repertoire of his memories needed major renovations after fourteen years of grandma's passing. Grandpa's mind never settled with living anywhere else in Lagos and opted to leave Lagos entirely. He relocated to his hometown, Fiditi in Oyo State, about two hours by road from Lagos. This further reduced my attraction to go to Lagos for university education. I opted to study medicine and applied to the University of Ibadan.

Still waiting for admission results, my dad came home one evening and excitedly told me 'Guess what? UI senate just approved that dentistry will be offered starting the next academic year'. I thought he was teasing me as he did sometimes. The next morning, he asked when I was going to the Admission Office and I asked him 'For what?' He repeated his message of the night before and this time, I was the excited one! Dentistry in Ibadan for real? I exclaimed!

In no time, I walked to the Admission Office, about a twenty-minute trek from our house on Lander Road on the UI campus, requesting a change in admission from medicine to dentistry. I faced many admissions officers, each asking me to defend my request. I was asked to write a statement and state the reasons why I did not apply to the dental school at the University of Lagos if I was as interested in dentistry as I claimed. I had my answers ready.

I tried to follow up with the Admission Office, but it stonewalled. I was told to wait for my letter in the mail. I impatiently awaited the decision on my admission request and would visit the Central Porter's Lodge on UI campus (the mail distribution center) every day to collect letters, hoping my letter would arrive. When I finally held in my hands, the admission letter to the University of Ibadan, Ibadan, Nigeria to be part of the pioneer dental class, it was a double-edged sword. I was thrilled about my admission but also sad within me.

This was a moment I wished my mother was there to share. It seemed ironic that I was going to study dentistry and, at the University of Ibadan where we lived but, mom was never going to know that. I could picture her excitement, the hugs that I would not get to feel and the lectures that would follow about what to do and not to do in university. Alas, the visits she had planned to make when I got to university would never materialize.

I cried for a while till dad decided to celebrate at the piano and called me to join him to sing songs of praise, thanking God for my admission. He was surely relieved that I got my wish to study dentistry. By the time we finished singing and had dinner, I felt calmer, anticipating university life and dental school days. My dad was pleased about my admission to study dentistry. He saw it as a silver lining amidst our grief and sorrow. He encouraged me to share that frame of mind.

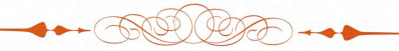

## CHAPTER III:

# THE SOJOURN THROUGH THE UNIVERSITY OF IBADAN DENTAL SCHOOL: 1975 -1980

In September 1975, I enrolled at the University of Ibadan Dental School in Ibadan, Nigeria with some of the most brilliant and gifted people I ever met. Relative to our peers in medicine, the dental class was a small cohort. Dentistry was a new program and we dental students were each, our brother's, or sister's keeper as we plodded through our preclinical and clinical years. We had the conviction that we were either going to sink or swim to safety together. We were a team, each team member holding tight to the lifeline towards the Bachelor of Dental Surgery (BDS) degree.

<u>Pre-Clinical Years</u>

Initially, dental students were indistinguishable from the medical students. The anatomy lectures and dissection laboratory sessions were the same for both medical and dental students for more than a year during which we dental students felt incognito. It was almost fifteen months into the program when Professor Schwartz came as a visiting lecturer and gave the dental class separate sessions in oral anatomy and histology. Physiology also had few lectures specific to oral tissues in addition to the whole body. Biochemistry did not offer any oral-specific lectures, simply kept the same scope of topics for both dental and medical students.

We were pioneers, our teachers were pioneers and dental curriculum, being the first, required streamlining. While as students, we did not know what we should be taught, we were not oblivious to what appeared to be uncertainty from the professors regarding the didactics they needed to engage with to prepare us for clinical dentistry. I was frustrated about this for a while and considered changing to the University of Lagos, which had a more established dental program. Again, family considerations in addition to a budding romantic relationship kept me from leaving Ibadan.

After the first year, I got a summer job with the Dental Service of the Western State of Nigeria for three months from June to September 1976 and was posted to Adeoyo Dental Clinic in Ibadan. This allowed me to shadow Dr. Adeniran. In addition to watching him at the Adeoyo clinic, I also travelled with him to the Dental Clinic in Oyo, which was located about fifty miles northwest of Ibadan. This was about a sixty-minute drive one way.

Dr. Adeniran guided me in examining dental patients and recognizing some signs of dental diseases. I watched him do fillings and extractions and refer cases beyond the scope of the clinic to secondary and tertiary dental centers as he explained the limitations that precluded him from treating the referred patient. Patients came from many neighboring towns, some travelling for hours and in pain. The need for dental service was immense and availability of care was limited to a four-hour slot in a week. Our stops to eat on our way back was a special treat that I looked forward to each week.

As my summer immersion continued, Dr. Adeniran encouraged me to attempt taking alginate impressions on staff members who were willing and, he would critique these for me. I watched the Dental Hygienists and Dental Assistants at each location and assisted them as allowed. I was also able to sit beside the Dental Technologist as he set up partial and full dentures. This summer immersion in clinical dentistry settled my choice for dentistry and from then on, there was no looking back.

By the time it was time to go back to school in September, the frustrations of the first year had ebbed and I became expectant of the clinical years. I told myself, 'I just need to ride out the rest of the pre-clinical period and then, I would be focusing on dentistry'. This frame of mind was motivating and encouraging. It helped me focus on preparing for the Part I BDS examination five months later. Unfortunately, I passed only two thirds of the first examination (anatomy and biochemistry) and failed physiology. I was sorely disappointed with myself but knew I needed to keep going.

I was faced with a tri-juggle for three months after the first examination. Firstly, I needed to take remedial classes in physiology at the University of Ibadan main campus (UI) to increase the probability of passing my re-sit examination. Secondly, I needed to attend with my assigned group, the sessions on Introduction to the Clinics at the University College Hospital Ibadan (UCH) which is about thirty minutes by car from UI main campus when traffic is uncongested. If I did not, I would be dropped from the clinical group and that would edge me out of the specialty rotations expected to follow about nine months later. Thirdly, the classes that would get dental students ready for clinical dentistry were also beginning at the new location for the Dental School in the same timeframe.

Even though the Dental School was across from the hospital, the sequence of the classes each day was different. UI classes were usually in the morning, but laboratory sessions were often in the afternoon. UCH and Dental School classes were sometimes in between UI classes, and I had to go back and forth the three locations more than once on some days. In addition. I was hopping on one leg; the other had a broken ankle in cast. I would surely be late to my classes if had to go on foot even if my Dental School classes were immediate to my UCH classes or vice versa. Yet, if I did not attend the pre-clinical dental classes, I would lose placement in my class for the Part II and Part III of the BDS program and be edged out of the clinical dental phase that I could not wait to get to. The tri-juggle made me very anxious. I was not confident that I could successfully complete all three activities simultaneously and progress to the next phase. I shuddered at my plight should I fail at one of my tri-juggle events. The probability of failing at all three was scary and almost paralyzed my mind. However, the fear of not graduating from dental school was the propel that kept me going.

I should talk about my broken ankle, another event of teachable moments. Soon after my failed BDS Part I examination, I attended a student political activity organized on campus in which there was stampede and my right ankle got broken. I was too scared to call and let my dad know I was injured and could not go home due to immobilization from my broken ankle. He was aware of the student demonstration as we lived on the university campus and after a sleepless night worrying about me, dad came to my hostel to check on me the next morning. Usually, he would send me a message and I would go and meet him at the gate but, this time, I was carried to his car by a friend since I could not walk on my own.

He took me straight to the university medical clinic also known as JAJA CLINIC where the attending medical staff put my ankle in a cast. I got medical care all right and, also got a copious dose of dad's displeasure at my behavior. He let me know in noticeably clear terms that the physical injuries I sustained were self-inflicted because of my decision to attend a political rally when I should be studying for my re-sit examination. He was not sympathetic to my predicament at all. I earned a grave reprimand from him but, dad still made available provisions for me to undertake my tri-juggle. He provided a dedicated driver to get me to my three locations as needed. There was no way I could have gotten my commute done without the transportation arrangements he made. Without his support and tough love, I could not have completed the requirements for me to advance to the clinical phase of the dentistry program. I will ever be grateful for that.

<u>Clinical Years</u>

After successfully passing the re-sit examination, I was able to advance to Part II of the BDS program. The first part featured lectures in Pharmacology and Pathology. Dental students were still assimilated amidst medical students but, the lecturers were beginning to pay the dental students the attention they deemed fit. From time to time, each pathology lecturer highlighted what was unique or impactful to dental tissues from general body pathology. Pharmacology lecturers highlighted the impacts of drugs that increased or reduced salivation and possible challenges that these could present for the dentist.

The preclinical sessions in Dental Laboratory Mechanics, Operative Techniques and Science of Dental Materials were held in the new dental laboratory. It was an environment that gave us students a feeling of euphoria, provided divergence from medical peers and increased our motivation. Anticipation of the next phase, when our clinical sessions would be centered around the orofacial tissues was very palpable in the air and this was exciting for all dental students. I felt settled with my choice of dentistry, ready to take on the clinical aspect whose preview I got through the summer immersion I had with Dr. Adeniran. That summer experience was indeed a buckeye seed for me.

Part III of the BDS program featured the last two and half years of our dental education, dedicated to oral care, in a building with brand new dental equipments. Our faculty members poured themselves into our education with immense devotion and commitment. Professor Daramola, JOD as we called him, and the late Professor Ajagbe were the first two dental faculty members to be appointed. Although Oral Surgery was the specialty for both, they provided information on all dental specialties to give us preliminary understanding.

JOD was the Head of the newly created Department of Dentistry at the College of Medicine of the University of Ibadan. We students watched him juggle teaching and establishing the dental program. He was the face of dentistry to us students as he was to his medical colleagues. He carried all the burden of dentistry on his shoulders with unimaginable resilience and determination. As the Class Representative in clinical years, I was in his office many times, expressing the frustration that the students felt as best as I could.

Ever the gentleman and self-assured person, he always listened intently. His cool demeanor never failed to calm and reassure me and all the students that all the concerns expressed will be addressed. He would always state that he was confident that all the problems we had then would be solved. He was indeed the selfless leader and soothsayer into the future of every dental student who passed through the University of Ibadan Dental School.

We still had classes with medical students in Medicine and Surgery and the faculty members tried to emphasize what they thought was peculiar to the mouth or pertinent to the orofacial tissues. I remember the lecture on oral clefts and how Professor Oluwasanmi addressed it with mastery, enlightening us that the dentist has a lot to do with avoiding 'failure of the infant to thrive'. This, he said was essential to preparing the infant for surgery before he as a plastic surgeon could close the cleft defect. This may partly underlie my attraction to study factors affecting oral cleft both for the thesis for my master's degree in public health and doctoral dissertation in later years.

The otorhinolaryngologists and ophthalmologists, Ear, Nose and Throat (ENT) and Eye specialists respectively, acknowledged that they share the same domain of operation with dentists and stressed the need for collaboration between their specialties and dentistry. The structure of the dental curriculum was becoming established and more organized and, hope was rising among the dental students.

By the Fall of 1977, clinical dentistry had employed additional staff. There was Dr. Luthra for Prosthodontics, Dr. Kulasekara for Periodontics and Dr. Noah for Pedodontics. We also had Associate Lecturers from the Western State Dental Service (WSDS) in the person of Dr. Adewunmi who taught Orthodontics, Dr. Ajayi-Obe and Dr. Olaniyan also from WSDS along with Dr. Aremu from the Baptist Dental Center in Ibadan. All three taught Restorative Dentistry. Professor Mosadomi came as a Visiting Lecturer from the University of Lagos to teach Oral Pathology.

Then, the twins, Dr. D.O. Lawoyin and Dr. J.O. Lawoyin both came in with zest, wit, passion, directness, youthfulness, and humor. Professionally astute, they quickly infused their professionalism in the students. They brought dentistry alive to us and encouraged each one of us to strive for excellence. They were charismatic and had an amazing energy that motivated the students. Other trailblazers were Registrars in Dentistry in the persons of Dr. Bode Falomo, Dr. Dickson Ufomata, Dr. Tosanwunmi, Dr. Lanre Bello, all in Restorative Dentistry and Dr. Dapo Abiose in Oral Surgery. They were all immensely helpful to us in the clinic and contributed to our success.

Clinical sessions ran continuously, and each dental student experienced providing patient care in the different specialties under faculty supervision. By the time we were in fourth year, my classmates and I were all settled into the dental school. We worked together, each of us attempting to meet the requirements set for graduation. We helped one another to reach the goal. Once one of us met the requirement for a specialty, he or she willingly reached out to the others to see who still needed patients with the specific criteria. My dental class remained a cohesive team.

It was all hands-on deck for the dental faculty, staff from the dental laboratory, the nursing staff, the dental hygienists, and the dental assistants to get the pioneer dental class to the finish line. They were as anxious as we students and we were blessed with their unyielding support. My deep gratitude to my dad, family, and family friends for their unrelenting care through dental school and beyond. Of special mention are Chief and Mrs. Femi Atanda, Mrs. Morin Soremi and Mrs. Bisola Balogun.

At the swearing-in ceremony, Professor Oluwole Akande, who was the Provost of the College of Medicine remarked that the 1980 ceremony was historic; being the first swearing-in ceremony held at the College of Medicine for Medical and Dental graduates. As I gave the valedictory address on behalf of the class in June 1980, it was bitter-sweet to have to part with those with whom I held hands for all of five years. Although we studied and mingled together for five years, each of us was undoubtedly ready to earn the Bachelor of Dental Surgery (BDS) degree of the University of Ibadan, Ibadan, Nigeria and fly in different directions.

*1975- First year of Dental School at the University of Ibadan, Ibadan, Nigeria.*

*1980 – Graduating from Dental School at the University of Ibadan, Ibadan, Nigeria.*

## CHAPTER IV:

# BEYOND THE UNIVERSITY OF IBADAN DENTAL SCHOOL

My journey since graduating from the University of Ibadan Dental School in 1980 is narrated in sections. Each section features a decade of my professional life with few overlaps between the decades.

<table>
<tr><td>1980-1990</td><td>1991-2000</td></tr>
<tr><td colspan="2" style="text-align:center">Four Decades in the Dental Profession</td></tr>
<tr><td>2001-2010</td><td>2011-2020</td></tr>
</table>

The first decade features my experience at the different institutions where I had the privilege of obtaining additional training and or serving. Later decades may present less distinction between places of service but, each features the different activities that characterized the decade.

# Beyond the University of Ibadan Dental School
## Section 1: 1980-1990

<u>University College Hospital (UCH) Dental Center, Oritamefa, Ibadan, Nigeria</u>

Following graduation in 1980, I remained at my alma mater, University of Ibadan Dental School for the Housemanship year and served as a Dental House Officer at the Dental Center of the University College Hospital (UCH) in Oritamefa, Ibadan, Nigeria. Rotating through the different departments allowed me to figure out my interests. Restorative Dentistry was fascinating, but my artistry skill was only rudimentary. I barely survived clinical prosthodontics, even though I enjoyed the laboratory aspect. I knew I was not created with enough patience to cope with Pedodontics long-term and, I was not a good fit for Periodontology.

Oral Surgery (OS) posting was exciting to me in the clinic and especially in the theatre where I could scrub and assist on some cases under the watch of our dedicated teachers Professor Daramola, Professor Ajagbe and Dr. D. Lawoyin. The post-operative difference in oral clefts and ameloblastoma cases were intriguing and the post-surgical care provided great learning opportunities for me. I slowly gained confidence in handling simple jaw fractures when on call and became increasingly audacious with third molar extractions. I strongly considered Oral Surgery for specialty but, my attraction to Orthodontics prevailed.

While in dental school, I had the opportunity to treat under Dr. Adewunmi's guidance, eight-year-old Alice who refused to smile because her upper right central incisor (front tooth) was in crossbite (upper behind the lower). In contrast, the upper left central incisor was buccally positioned and proclined (bucked). Using the tongue blade to apply labial pressure to the tooth, Alice's upper right incisor came out of crossbite after a few weeks and set the transformation in this little girl. Four months earlier, she would not talk to anyone and getting her to open her mouth for an oral examination was a challenge. Suddenly, Alice would talk to me incessantly about school, her friends and brother. Her self-confidence improved tremendously. The introvert in her crawled out of its shell as soon as her upper right front tooth translated to a more forward position.

Dr. Adewunmi directed me to go one step further and asked me to construct a Hawley appliance to move her upper left central incisor lingually (back) and align both incisors. She had me read up on the different components to gain understanding of what was to be achieved. She then worked on the design with me as I learnt to bend the C clasp, the T loop, Adam's clasp, Z spring and the labial bow. Under the guidance of Mr. Fasan and Mr. Idowu in the dental laboratory, I learnt to pour and cure the acrylic that kept all the components together and produce the appliance. The appliance was delivered to Alice for full time wear and thereafter, I saw her for monthly visits for activation.

Within a few months of wearing the appliance, Alice bloomed with self-esteem and the shy, withdrawn girl, exploded with uninhibited enthusiasm and self-confidence. Her mom reported that her teacher had remarked on Alice becoming more interactive in class and with her peers as her teeth improved. I could only marvel at the impact that rearranging her teeth with a removable orthodontic appliance had on her inner joy in the twelve months I treated her. I imagined how her new confidence would defeat previous inhibitions and empower her to tackle the future.

The case of Alice remained with me, highlighting the effect of malocclusion not only on oral function, but also the perception of self both by the patient and by others. It set my trajectory to orthodontics as a career for the last thirty-six years and counting.

By the time I finished my housemanship year, I had decided that wire-bending and teeth straightening were in the cards for me. I started looking into options to study orthodontics as a specialty both in the United Kingdom (UK) and the United States of America (USA). Professor Daramola encouraged me to pursue graduate education in the United Kingdom and gave me information to obtain preparatory materials for the Part I fellowship examination. I also looked at several schools in the USA where my fiancé was pursuing his doctoral program. Case Western Reserve University in Cleveland, Ohio piqued my interest, not only for its orthodontic program, but also for the Bolton Brush Craniofacial collection. I applied to Case Western Reserve University to study orthodontics and while on vacation, followed up with a visit to Cleveland, Ohio at the end of my housemanship year. Professor Donald Enlow who was then the Chair of the Department was very welcoming as were other members of the orthodontic department. I was looking forward to studying there the following year.

### Lagos University Teaching Hospital (LUTH) in Idi Araba, Lagos, Nigeria.

Following my housemanship year, I served at the Lagos University Teaching Hospital (LUTH) in Idi Araba, Lagos, Nigeria for the National Youth Service Corps (NYSC) year. This is a one-year compulsory service for every graduate in Nigeria up till now. It is an opportunity to go to an area of the country that is relatively new to the graduate for cultural immersion while operating at the grass roots with the skills learned in the university.

At my welcome session with Professor Adenubi, who was the Head of Child Oral Health Department under whose umbrella Orthodontics laid, I was asked for my interests and prospective graduate plans. I expressed interest in orthodontics and was thus assigned to the Orthodontic Clinic. There, I got my initiation to fixed appliance therapy using the Begg Technique under the tutelage of Professor Isikwe. I watched Dr. Ayo Soyombo and other residents bond patients with Begg brackets as we all listened to Professor Isikwe recount his experiences under Dr. Logan and in Albuquerque, NM.

Outside the orthodontic clinic at LUTH, I got tutelage and support by many others. Professor Okoisor, Uncle Frank as I call him was a great calming force for my anxieties and fears. He would always tell me, 'Don't worry, I know you'll do well' and he followed up on my progress continuously after I left LUTH. I got a second dose of the Okoisor encouragement and support years later from his wife, Dr. (Mrs.) Adebola Okoisor (Aunty as I call her) when I worked with her briefly in Wadi Al Dawasir, Saudi Arabia. She was most loving to me and called me 'Omo Frank' (Frank's Child). Her pineapple crumble was always a lifter of the spirit as it was a sweetener to the mouth. You bet I never said no to it. I remember her each time I try her recipe.

Similarly, Professor Mosadomi, who came to Ibadan from LUTH to teach us Oral Pathology when I was a dental student was kind to me when I was at LUTH. He would always ask how I was settling in LUTH each time our paths crossed. His wife, Mrs. Adewunmi Mosadomi who I met years later when I worked in Riyadh, Saudi Arabia is a fascinating, loving and cheerful person. I never had a dull moment with her and, she often had words of wisdom to share. Dr. Tola Roberts, whom I knew through Dr Adewunmi was also of great support while I was at LUTH, constantly encouraging me to keep advancing in my chosen specialty.

Professor J.O. Adenubi with his cool self and unique sense of humor was a great inspiration to my graduate dental education. While I was at LUTH, he told me that if I decided to go to the USA, the only school he wanted to see me get graduate education was the University of Michigan, referred to as U of M. Even after I told him I already had acceptance to Case Western University in Cleveland, Ohio, over and over, his message of "Michigan it is" did not change. Out of curiosity, I looked up this 'U of M' and its acceptance rate was not encouraging. However, it had a Center for Human Growth and Development and that made me decide to apply. Alas, I not only got a rejection letter, but was told not to bother to apply to the University of Michigan in the future with the grades I had. I was sad, dumbfounded and confused.

I discussed my rejection from U of M with Professor Adenubi and, he simply smiled as he usually did and told me 'There must be some miscommunication somewhere. You are one of the best students in your class and I know you will not let this defeat you.' After recovering from my initial disappointment, my reaction was not to bother about U of M since I already got admission to Case Western Reserve University in Ohio, visited there and liked the environment. However, my fighter spirit evolved, and I had to find out possible reasons for the rejection and take steps to fight it.

I learnt for the first time about the difference in the grading system between our dental school and schools in the USA. In Nigeria, the closed marking system is used, which has seventy percent as its upper limit and the threshold for distinction. On the other hand, in the USA, seventy percent is a C-grade and is not acceptable for graduate studies. I was not sure that this was the reason for denying me admission. Nevertheless, this information helped me understand what I needed to focus on to request a review of my admission denial from the University of Michigan.

On further inquiries, I found out about the World Education Service that would translate transcripts relative to the standards used in each country. I was aware that U of M had graduate dental students from Nigeria but, I was not sure if they had their transcripts translated. I decided that getting my transcript translated would be additional information to accompany my admission review request. This seemed vital for transcript interpretation and evaluation. My husband at the time was pursuing his graduate study at the University of Wisconsin, Madison, WI. He recommended that I should request my class ranking in every subject to show my relative performance in the class. This appeared to be a more dentistry-specific transcript translation personalized to me. I decided to pursue this option as additional information to attach to the request for a review of my admission decision.

While on a family visit to Ibadan, I stopped by my alma mater to see Professor Daramola, who was still the Head of the Department of Dentistry. When I told him about my rejection letter from U of M, he expressed surprise. I shared with him my plan to request a review of the admission decision and requested for my class ranking in every examination taken while at the dental school. He prepared this for every subject covered in all BDS examinations. He also attached the list of the prizes for my class which showed that I got both the Class prize and the V.D.F. Oki's prize in Oral Surgery. These accompanied my letter to U of M requesting a review of the decision on my admission for graduate orthodontics. Soon after U of M received the request, I got the letter reversing the previous admission decision. Professor Daramola's advocacy and support was pivotal to my admission for graduate education in dentistry.

I debated for a while whether I should go to U of M or Case Western Reserve University. The latter was my first admission and where I had a pleasant and welcoming visit. After a lot of deliberations, I bought into the Michigan challenge despite my pre-admission experience. That experience let me know that I needed to get to the University of Michigan running on both feet.

Once I informed Professor Adenubi of my decision to go to U of M, he told me, "I knew you would fight it out" and then contacted Dr. Lanre Bello, one of his protégées who was a resident in Pedodontics at U of M to look out for me. Dr. Bello helped me navigate U of M and his entire family was most hospitable to me in Ann Arbor, MI.

My LUTH experience would not be complete without mention of my childhood friend, Professor Mobolanle Olugbemiga Ogunlewe. She went beyond friendship to support me while I worked as an NYSC Dentist at LUTH, and she was serving as a Dental House Officer at the same institution. I did not immediately get accommodation on campus and given the traffic between LUTH and Ikeja where my brother lived, commuting would have been arduous for my pregnant self. Professor Ogunlewe offered that I share her accommodation until mine was assigned. In no time, I became the landlady and she, the tenant. She selflessly took measures to make sure I was comfortable. When my LUTH accommodation was later assigned about four months into the NYSC year, fellowshipping with her precluded my moving. We both shared her apartment for the entire year and I was surely the beneficiary.

She was kind and generous both with her materials and in her spirit. Her hospitality made my stay at LUTH unforgettable. Being a colleague in dentistry, professionally, we were each other's sounding board. We would discuss our experiences each day and brainstorm on plans for graduate studies. She was pursuing oral surgery which was one of my considerations for specialty training. It was enlightening to discuss some of the cases she managed during her rotations. I will always be grateful for her support then and in the years beyond. Till this day, she remains a selfless friend.

Back to the Alma Mater Part I: Dental Research Fellow

Having decided to move back to Ibadan following NYSC to be around family for my first baby, I applied for a Senior Dental House Officer position with the University College Hospital (UCH) and Oyo State Government Dental Service. Dr. Toyin Fafowora, Thompson then, who was my roommate at Alexander Brown Hall in the last two years of dental school came to visit and shared the news that she had just received her letter of employment with UCH and that mine was also ready for pick up. Once I received the joint employment letter from the University College Hospital Dental Center and the College of Medicine of the University of Ibadan, the die was cast against Oyo State Government Dental Service.

Shortly after I started work, the University of Ibadan Dental School initiated a Staff Development Program and, I was appointed as a Dental Research Fellow with the College of Medicine. My admission for graduate orthodontics gave me eligibility to be one of the first recipients of the program to leave for graduate dental education. The program funded my orthodontic program at the University of Michigan.

My deepest gratitude to the College of Medicine of the University of Ibadan for the sponsorship. This is a privilege that I do not take for granted. It was surely God's blessing that set me up for future opportunities that have enriched my professional life.

The University of Michigan, Ann Arbor, MI. Part I - Orthodontic Specialty Training

I arrived at the University of Michigan with some anxiety from my admission process and the challenge that it posed as a tough school. The anxiety only worsened when on my first day, I was summoned to the office of Dean of Students as I signed in. My mind was in a whirlwind, wondering what trouble was waiting for me. However, those fears were quickly put at ease when the Dean welcomed me to Ann-Arbor and wished me well at the school. I breathed a sigh of relief after talking to the Dean and determined that I must focus on whatever it would take for me to succeed at the University of Michigan School of Dentistry.

I was the only female and non-American in my orthodontic class of eight. I had a lot to learn amidst my seasoned colleagues, many of whom had been in general dental practice for many years before deciding to undertake graduate education in orthodontics. They were all extremely helpful to me and I, un-hesitantly tapped into their experience. Thankfully, U of M had a Learning Center in the basement of the School of Dentistry. It housed videotapes of every procedure performed at the school and recordings of all the lectures covered in each subject in every specialty offered at the school. This facility allows each person to remediate as needed. The library on the third floor was equally informative and these two became my haven.

With time, I overcame my anxieties and completed everything I needed to succeed in didactics and clinical management of patients. The students were each exposed to many clinical instructors, most of whom had their private practices in Ann Arbor and neighboring cities. They all brought in their clinical experience, practice philosophies and modalities. Patients assigned to the students were supervised by the different instructors and it was enriching to learn how different instructors treated similar cases. All the teachers in graduate orthodontics impacted my specialty training. Of special mention are Dr. Surrender Nanda and Dr. Peter Vig, who were the respective Orthodontic

Chairperson during my first and second years of residency. I am grateful to them all and to the orthodontic staff supporting faculty and students - Ms. Delores Ramsey, Ms. Debbie Stambaugh and Ms. Joyce Gunnell.

While at U of M, I got to study orthodontics and more. I got excited with the research designs taught and spent some time with Dr. Walker who encouraged me to prepare my thesis proposal early. By the end of my second semester, I had my research plan well laid out and approached Dr. Moyers at the U of M Center for Human Growth and Development to be my Thesis Committee Chair. With his guidance, my research proposal was completed and approved. With that approval, I was able to obtain a travel grant that funded my trip to Nigeria to collect the data needed for my master's thesis.

My heartfelt thanks to my parents in law, Chief and Mrs. S.S. Fatunde of blessed memory for taking care of my daughter during my orthodontic residency and for their kindness to me throughout.

# GRADUATE ORTHODONTICS
## CLASS OF 1984

BOOKWALTER, GREGG

COKER, JOHN

EVANS, LARRY

FATUNDE, ADEJOKE

GANZ, DANIEL

JOSEPH, WAYNE

SIOMKA, LEON

WRIGHT, WILLIAM

*University of Michigan, Ann Arbor, MI. USA - Orthodontic Graduating Class of 1984*

In my second year of orthodontic residency, I had the opportunity to work as a Research Assistant to Dr. Robert Moyers. He was at the time, the Director of the U of M Center for Human Growth and Development (CHGD) which features faculty members from different specialties in dentistry, medicine, public health, psychology, anthropology, and social work. I got exposure to craniofacial growth data and worked directly with Bob Wainwright, the statistician, and a genius at his trade. Dr. Jim McNamara and his experiments with monkeys on Class II malocclusion correction were fascinating to me as I studied craniofacial growth.

Then, there was Dr. Stanley Garn, a faculty member and anthropologist for whom writing articles was like drinking water. He had a party celebrating every hundredth article he published. I attended two of his parties at U of M and wondered, 'how on earth is anyone able to write so many articles?' In my study of ectodermal cells, I read some of his articles on teeth and hair that were written before 1958. I chose to question him on these. I was dumbfounded to see how engaged he was discussing these articles almost thirty years later. I expressed my respect for his level of engagement in articles written that far back, even before I was born. His response was 'Before I write anything, it is conceptualized and developed in my mind. Writing it, is simply photographing my mind where it all stays for as long as I am waking and walking'. By the time I left U of M, he had written over seven hundred published scholastic articles. U of M encouraged such distinguished scholarliness.

Dr. Moyers was not only my boss, supervisor, and thesis chair, he was indeed a fatherly figure. He refused to let me be complacent and was always ready to push me to the next level. At his directive, I took courses outside of the orthodontic department in anthropology, genetics and public health. Those helped my understanding of growth of the human skull even beyond childhood. He also encouraged me to sign up for a doctoral program in Human Growth and Development. The courses I had taken outside of the dental school were applicable and I got admission to a multi-disciplinary doctoral program in Human Growth and Development.

After completing my M.S. degree in Orthodontics, I served as a Clinical Instructor at U of M Orthodontics Department for the next eighteen months. With this came the opportunity to obtain a Michigan State dental license limited to operations within the dental school. Remaining in Ann Arbor after my orthodontic program allowed me to continue with the classes needed for my doctoral program.

Once I finished the course work, I took the preliminary examination also known as the qualifying examination but did not pass. It was time to return to Nigeria to serve my bond at the University of Ibadan Dental School and I planned to work on the research phase of my doctoral program once I got back to Nigeria. Unfortunately, this was stalled since starting the research project was contingent on passing the preliminary examination. After a second attempt and still not passing the qualifying examination, I decided to give up the doctoral program. This was a tough decision.

I have dealt with needing to retake examinations before but, giving up on something I set out to do, was unusual for me. I agonized over this but, I had to face reality. I was back in Nigeria and did not have available, all the resources I needed for remediation to ensure increased probability that I would pass at the next attempt of the qualifying examination. I knew I had limited number of times to attempt the examination and did not want to try without increased likelihood of success. Reluctantly, I decided it was prudent to walk away from the doctoral program.

## Back at the Alma Mater Part II: Faculty Teaching Orthodontics

I returned to the University of Ibadan Dental School in December 1985 and served as a Lecturer in Orthodontics until November 1988. During that time, I taught didactic and laboratory orthodontics to dental students and developed the orthodontic curriculum. I also established the protocol for running the orthodontic clinic and held clinic sessions for students on Monday afternoons.

Professor Gbemisola Oke, then Aderinokun had her office opposite mine at the clinic's end and we frequently shared our thoughts. Professor Oke's life is very inspiring to me. She is known to be undaunted in taking on tasks and challenges. I was mesmerized when she produced the design for a non-electric dental chair, got it constructed and unveiled at the Nigerian Dental Association meeting. What ingenuity! It was truly refreshing to see a colleague conceptualize solutions to problems in a contextual manner, looking within and using materials that are locally available to address needs effectively.

After the conference, the dental chair stayed between our two offices for a while and later became the incentive that led us to establish the Idikan Community Dental Clinic as an outreach of the University of Ibadan Dental School. Professor Oke and I worked at this clinic on Tuesday and Thursday mornings, running the clinic primarily with our personal funds.

This experience stuck a chord that awakened the dental public health nerves within me. I remembered the unmet dental needs during my summer immersion. I also recalled some of the activities of the Nigerian Dental Students Association for which I served as Secretary. I noted that I enjoyed the school visits by dental students to give oral health education sessions to elementary school students and their teachers. I began to wonder on how best to reach the non-patient population who may not come to the dental school or dental clinic for treatment.

My Eastward Movement Part I:

In November 1988, I got the itchy feet, took leave of absence to go east and work for two years as an Orthodontist at the Riyadh Dental Center in Riyadh, the capital of Saudi Arabia. The work week was from Saturday to Thursday, and it took a while for me to adjust to working on Saturday and Sunday. Schools ran from Saturday to Wednesday for the children but, they adjusted very quickly. It was city living in Riyadh, with many stores available in the western world within reach. That was a pleasant surprise within the middle east context in my mind.

Women were not allowed to drive and were required to be accompanied by male relatives. Alas, my male relative was my three-year-old son! Needing to be bused to work and shopping was a new experience. Outside of these two activities, I had no provision for going elsewhere with my children. It took some time before I resigned myself to this limitation to my movement. However, I got help getting around Riyadh with my children from families. I am grateful to the Adeyokunnu, Mosadomi, Roberts, Adelusi, Irubo and Tetteh families for their fellowship and assistance to my family in the commute around Riyadh. Knowing I had help to get myself and my children around as needed was immeasurable support in a country where I could not drive. My heartfelt thanks also to Ruth for her help in taking care of the children. These allowed me the peace of mind to focus on my work.

I learnt about the Arabian culture, and struggled to understand why women needed to be veiled, always have a scarf over their heads and be chaperoned by male relatives. As a non-indigene, I could not understand why females would be clad in all black in the elevated temperature environment and risk continuous increase in body temperature. I could not fathom why they could not have their faces open to behold the scenery and all that was around them. On the other hand, my female colleagues in dentistry who were indigenes were in tune with these practices and explained to me that it showed that the males in the family have taken up the responsibility to protect their females who were deemed to be weaker and unable to defend themselves. The question-and-answer sessions with my colleagues were regular features of our lunch hour from which I learned cultural accommodation.

I communicated with my patients and their parents through the interpreters. Clinically, I learnt to seek to understand reasons behind patients' choices and perspectives. Each clinic session was an opportunity for interaction with patients and their families and a forum for continued cultural education that needed to be considered in treatment. I began to appreciate why some patients or parents were insistent on closing diastemas (spaces) between anterior teeth, especially on the females. This was contrary to my experience with other cultures where people paid to have diastemas created between their teeth, especially the front teeth. The space between the front teeth was perceived as an element of beauty within the cultural environment of the latter.

The uniqueness of working in Saudi Arabia was the opportunity to work with colleagues from different countries and interact with people of diverse cultures worldwide. I mingled with indigenes of Saudi Arabia and African countries including Ghana, Egypt, Eritrea, Kenya and Nigeria. I learnt about diversity within the African continent itself. There were colleagues and staff from India, Pakistan, China and western countries in Europe and North America. Simply put, working in Saudi Arabia gave me a United Nations experience.

Ramadan was a unique experience, featuring a reversal of time in Saudi Arabia. Though Ramadan is also observed by Muslims in my home country Nigeria, the work hours of the day remain the same, 8a-4.30p across all seasons and festivities. In Saudi Arabia, during Ramadan, we worked split hours, longer shift at night 9p-2a, after the fast would have been broken in addition to a shorter than normal morning shift 9a-12noon.

Scheduling orthodontic procedures had to reflect the Ramadan effect. The morning shift was characterized by poor patient turn out or 'no show' since the fast prohibits Muslims from drinking water or eating during the day. On the contrary, during the evening shift which sometimes lasted till 2am or 3am, patients were more alert, having been infused with energy from the meals eaten when their fast was broken. Efficient and effective patient scheduling required orthodontic procedures that needed longer time to be scheduled during the night shift while the morning shift was reserved mainly for emergencies and short procedures. I cherish the Middle East experience for its diversity in both patient and non-patient interactions.

With the gulf war looming, I had a lot of concern about my ability to protect my three little children amidst the impending need to wear gas masks and all needed gears in a setting where I was not allowed to drive. Just before the Gulf War started, I relocated with our children to the United States of America in 1990 to join my husband.

# Beyond the University of Ibadan Dental School
## Section 2: 1991-2000

I came back to the USA from the Middle East at a time when getting a job as a dentist was like finding a needle in the haystack. The United States at that time, had just closed six dental schools for what appeared to be an 'overproduction' of dentists. There were the stringiest restrictions to foreign trained dentists wanting to practice dentistry in the United States. Irrespective of a graduate degree in a dental specialty from a USA accredited school, it was a USA dental degree (DDS or DMD) that ensured eligibility for dental licensure examinations in all states. This seemed to serve as a screening measure to combat the 'overproduction'. The dearth of opportunities on my return to the USA in 1990 was a wake-up call, but one which gave me a greater appreciation for the opportunities God had given me a-priori.

I served as a Research Fellow at the University of Pennsylvania (Penn), working on temporomandibular pain, commuting between Pennsylvania and Texas where my family lived. This sparked my interest in craniofacial pain and, I ventured into both the fellowship and mastership programs of the International College of Cranio-mandibular Orthopedics (ICCMO). While doing this, I also served as a volunteer at the Craniofacial Clinic at the University of Texas, Dental Branch in Houston, TX. Not sure when the licensure issue would be resolved, I started exploring opportunities in dental public health and made inquiries into obtaining a master's degree in Public Health (MPH).

I had passed both parts of the National Dental Board Examination which are pre-requisites for dental licensure examination. I also took the bench test as an initial step to licensure examinations in Washington DC but was yet to take the clinical examination. Not being able to roll the crystal ball into the future for my dental licensure, I considered going back to dental school for the DDS degree so I would be free to seek licensure wherever I wanted. I applied for the PASS program at Penn, which allows a foreign trained dentist to enroll in the last two years of dental school and thereafter obtain the United States dental degree to become eligible for licensure examinations. I enrolled in the mandatory summer program preceding the fall start of the PASS program. Just before the summer program ended, it became clear that none of the three sources of funding I hoped would support me through the program will materialize. With no funds to pay for the PASS program, I withdrew my admission and had to review my options.

My Eastward Movement Part II:

I went back to the Middle East to work as an Orthodontist at the Armed Forces Hospital in Wadi Al Dawasir, Saudi Arabia. There, I was contracted to initiate orthodontics services. However, the details needed to get the clinic going were yet to be finalized and the clinic initiation was rescheduled for a later date. I left after three months and accepted another Orthodontist position at the Al Baha Dental Center, which is associated with the Al Baha Hospital in Al Baha, Saudi Arabia. Dr. Farhan Al Saleh was the Director of the Al Baha Dental Center at the time.

Al-Baha, situated in the southwest gave me another view of Saudi Arabia that is different from Riyadh. The cultural environment was pretty much the same but, unlike Riyadh, it featured less influence of western culture. Compared to Riyadh, Al Baha was a smaller city, a Bedouin community for which the Al Baha Hospital is one of its main highlights. Its terrain features a diverse topography that includes valleys, plains, mountains, waterfalls, forests and the coastal plain of Tihama. With a relatively more temperate climate, it attracts tourists from the heat clad areas of Saudi Arabia and neighboring countries. Shopping, however, was limited to the Baljourashi market while occasional get out trips to Riyadh provided some excitement especially for the children. The hospital itself was very much self-contained, with the staff accommodations, a school for the children, and a supermarket within its campus.

However, the Al Baha Dental Center was outside the hospital campus, needing a short daily commute to work by bus organized by the hospital. Renilda Sapara from the Medical Records Department was of immense help in picking up the children from school and babysitting them while I was still at work. That allowed me the freedom to serve my patients as needed. Many of the staff with whom I worked were either of Saudi origin or from Arab speaking countries, African countries or the Philippines. Interaction with patients was also through the interpreters, some of whom were dental assistants or dental technicians.

I continued to pursue obtaining a dental license in the USA to increase my practice options. While working in Al Baha, I traveled to the USA to take licensure examinations. I was relieved to get my dental license in Washington DC. in 1996.

Returning to Orthodontic Practice in the USA

With a license to practice in Washington DC, I was able to get the Michigan dental license I obtained while I served as a Clinical Instructor at U of M converted to a full clinical license not limited to dental school setting. Dr. Wayne Joseph, one of my classmates at U of M who had a large practice in Michigan hired me to work in his practice as an Associate Orthodontist. That allowed me to get back into clinical orthodontics. I worked part time, for thirty-six months at his offices in Detroit, Southfield, and Inkster in Michigan State from May 1997 to September 2000. During that period, I commuted to Michigan weekly from Katy, Texas where we lived.

I continued working on my MPH degree while pursuing a Fellowship in Dental Public Health at the University of Texas, in Houston, TX. My week was divided between my public health programs Monday to Wednesday and every Wednesday evening, I flew to Detroit to treat orthodontic patients Thursday through Saturday and flew back home on Saturday after work. This was tough on my family.

Towards the end of the decade, hope was rising for non-USA dental degree holders to obtain dental license. The dentist to patient ratio allowed more states to offer dental licensure examinations with less restrictions. The State of Texas, where I lived however, only allowed the regional dental board examinations and did not reciprocate with other states like the State of Michigan did with Washington DC. As soon as the State of Texas allowed, I attempted the dental licensure examination of the Western Regional Examination Board (WREB). I took this exam three times and fell short for a variety of reasons which included inadequate preparation and likely, having too many irons in the fire at once.

Texas State Board of Dental Examiners mandated me to take a compulsory six-week preparatory course before I was allowed a fourth attempt at the WREB examination. Luckily, the University of Texas offered this course at its Dental Branch in Houston, TX., about thirty miles from Katy, TX. where my family lived. I had six weeks to do nothing but concentrate on preparation for the examination and this really did help. I also enjoyed being home every day for that entire period since I did not need to travel to work. I finally passed the WREB and obtained my Texas dental license in 2000. This was quite a blessing that allowed me to stop traveling and work in Texas where I lived.

# Beyond the University of Ibadan Dental School
## Section 3: 2001-2010

Now with a license to practice, I returned to Texas in September 2000 and worked briefly as an Orthodontist at the office of Dr. Elgin Wells in Houston, TX. where I had served as volunteer many years prior. Later that year, I joined the corporate Dental Service Organization (DSO) and served as an Orthodontist with Castle Dental Centers until 2003. I worked in five locations in the Dallas Fort Worth Metroplex and a sixth in Waco, TX. This was a new experience that required a lot of coordination of the 'mobile ortho team' as it moved from office to office.

Thereafter, I established Sunny Smiles Orthodontics and went solo into private practice for the rest of the decade and about half of the next. It was exciting to have my own business and be able to practice as I envisioned. I had patients with diverse malocclusions and was happy to take on the clinical challenges of resolving these. I engaged in emerging technological modalities using self-ligating brackets, lingual orthodontics, and aligner therapy in addition to standard fixed and removable orthodontic appliances.

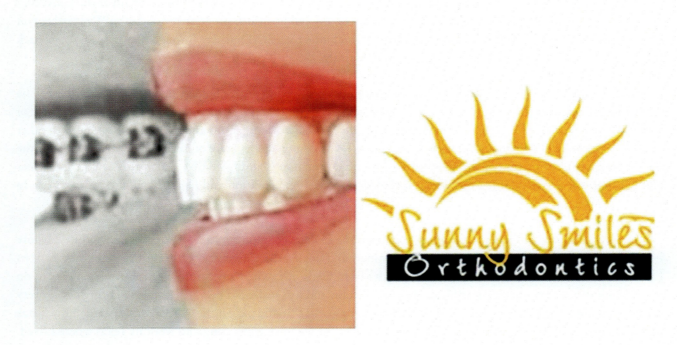

The administrative and marketing responsibilities of running a private clinic in an atmosphere of constantly changing regulations posed multi-layered challenges that sometimes served as distractions to patient care. Managing employees certainly was more involving than managing orthodontic team members with different teams that I worked with previously. After over ten years in private practice, I decided to hold on just to clinical care and relieve myself of the administrative and marketing burdens.

I sought opportunities to work at other clinics part time where my only responsibility was patient care. Simultaneously, I gradually wound down my private practice over a period of three years. This allowed me to complete orthodontic treatment for all the patients of record at Sunny Smiles Orthodontics.

Although I had completed the coursework for the MPH degree and the Fellowship in Dental Public Health by 2000, the research and field experience components were pending. I had just started the research phase of my MPH program when the Texas Birth Defects Registry initiated its surveillance program. This piqued my interest in oral cleft and for my MPH thesis, I studied the Association between Prenatal Alcohol and Tobacco Consumption and Oral Cleft among Infants born in Texas Region 6 and 11. I completed my MPH degree in 2001.

Completion of my Dental Public Health Fellowship however lingered for another three years partly because of my work schedule. During this period, the field experience associated with the fellowship program offered me exposure to the need of the dentally underserved in the USA. I got burdened for this target population of patients, not only in the USA, but in Nigeria and other countries. To address this growing burden within me, I inquired from the American Dental Association about volunteering opportunities and, I got more information than I imagined, reverberating how much need there is worldwide.

In December 2006, my entire family went to Saboba, Ghana to serve at the dental clinic of the Assemblies of God Church Hospital, the only health facility available to serve northern Ghana and neighboring areas in Togo at that time. It was a sobering experience for all of us to face how much need existed for dental service. From Ghana, my family headed to Nigeria, which allowed me to visit the Idikan Community Dental Clinic which had grown from the one room where we started in 1987. It was now located in a three room flat on the lower level of an adjacent newly built building.

Thanks to Professor Oke and her team of dedicated Community Dental Health Professionals; Professor Taiwo, Dr. Ibiyemi, Dr. Lawal, Dr. Osuh and other members of the team who continued to nurture and provide service at the clinic. Seeing the progress made at this clinic in almost twenty years since I worked there was great motivation for me to continue to seek avenues to increase access to dental care for those who could not afford it.

From my inquiries from the American Dental Association, I also learnt about the one-year fellowship of the Institute for Diversity and Leadership (IDL). I was denied admission the first two times I applied and was not going to apply again but my husband kept pushing me not to give up. On the third try, I got admitted to the IDL program for the 2007-2008 class. I learnt about health inequalities and the differential impacts of health policy on populations. Some of the factors that underlie the differential in health outcomes were identified. The challenge was to simulate viable solutions to the endless list of problems in different communities. Identifying the need(s) of each community, developing solution(s) to address the need(s), and evaluating the effectiveness of the proposed solution(s) were my takeaway from this program. IDL provided leadership tools and an invaluable networking environment.

At the end of the IDL Fellowship year, each person was required to present proposed solution(s) to problem(s) identified in a community of choice. For this, I focused on improving access to dental care for the underserved. Professor Oke, the co-founder of the Idikan Community Dental Clinic, was then the Dean of Dentistry at the University of Ibadan. She had plans to incorporate rural experience for dental students into the dental curriculum. I had plans to improve access to dental care in underserved communities.

Professor Oke joined me for my presentation at the final session of the IDL fellowship. We collaborated on our plans and, this led to the establishment of the Ibarapa Community Dental Clinic in 2008. It is located at the site of the Ibarapa Project in Igbo-Ora, Oyo State, Nigeria which is an outreach of the University of Ibadan Medical School. The clinic provides rural dentistry experience for dental students. With this, a new graduation requirement was introduced into the dental curriculum at the University of Ibadan Dental School. This requirement mandates each student to spend at least one month at the Ibarapa Community Dental Clinic. Residents and Fellows in Community Dentistry also rotate through the clinic. Usually, a team of three residents or fellows in the Department of Community Dentistry and ten dental students serve in each monthly rotation. This also became an avenue to implement my mission to improve access to dental care in underserved communities.

> *Ibarapa Community Dental Clinic Team on rotation featuring three Residents in Community Dentistry and ten Dental Students outside the Clinic with Supervising Faculty Professor Oke, seated center on the first row.*

In 2008, following the conclusion of the IDL fellowship, my next step in improving access to dental care was establishing Dental Outreach for Africa Inc. (DOFA), a 501c3 organization. It is a non-profit organization whose vision is to increase access to dental care in underserved communities. DOFA's mission is to bring dental care to the people by establishing community dental clinics within close proximity. The objective is to minimize factors that discourage or prevent patients from seeking preventive and restorative non-emergent dental care. These factors include conflict with work schedule, transportation cost, time to travel to clinics that are far, cost of dental care and other factors that may impact patients' decision to seek dental care timely. Under its umbrella, six community dental clinics have been established in Nigeria. Operations at the sixth and newest community dental clinic were scheduled to begin in 2021 but were delayed till March 2022 due to Covid-19. Services at the community dental clinics are provided in collaboration with dental schools.

The faculty and staff of the partnering institutions are to be commended for the daily operations and management of the clinics. Upper-class dental students, dental residents and fellows, under the supervision of faculty of the partnering dental school are the operators, providing dental care to the people in the communities.

The daily activities of each clinic are coordinated by the partnering institution. Collaborating with dental schools has been a key factor in ensuring continuation of dental service to the communities where DOFA clinics are located.

The operators on site include the dentist who must be a graduate of an accredited dental school and registered with the Nigerian Medical and Dental Council to practice dentistry. He or she may be a Dental House Officer, Youth Corp Dentist, a Dental Resident or Dental Fellow employed by the partnering institution.

The dentist on site oversees patient care and is in charge of the day-to-day activities of the clinic. In addition, he monitors the performance of the administrative staff (Appointment and Records Clerk) and clinical staff (Dental Assistant and Dental Hygienist) as well as Dental Students. He or she is also responsible for forwarding reports of the clinic to the Faculty in the Community Dentistry Department of the partnering institution. The faculty members make periodic visits to evaluate, teach and direct the staff and students to meet the objectives set for learning and outreach. The operations, supervision, and monitoring of the clinic's activities are under the administrative guideline of the partnering institution.

The team at each clinic go into the community to provide oral health education on prevention of dental diseases. This is accomplished during team visits to town hall meetings, schools, maternal and child health clinics, general health clinics and at the market. The goal is to educate members of the community about the relationship between oral health and general health. The message delivered is to encourage them to seek preventive dental care at the community dental clinic that exists in their locality.

Each clinic has a Community Liaison Officer (CLO) who is usually a community leader in a volunteering capacity. He or she acts as an ambassador, bringing the people's concern(s) regarding dental care to the clinic. He or she is also expected to disseminate information about dental services available at the clinic to the community. The CLO essentially helps to bridge communication gaps between the clinic and the community. He or she is expected to assist with propagating the outreach service of the clinic.

The focus of each DOFA clinic is oral health promotion, disease prevention and provision of primary dental care in a cost-effective manner. The clinics also serve as referral sources to secondary and tertiary institutions of dental service. DOFA helps with initial equipping and supplies for the first few years of each clinic. Thereafter, the clinic is expected to become self-sustaining. Patients are charged nominal fees on a sliding scale commensurate with their income. This provides funds that allow the clinics to be self-sustaining.

I serve as the Executive Director of DOFA, coordinating and monitoring the performance of the community dental clinics. I perform site reviews at least once a year, during which I also engage the staff for input regarding problems that they face and discuss solutions needed to assist effectively. During my visits, we often hold brainstorming sessions to continuously challenge the faculty at the academic level and staff of the clinics at grassroot level to discuss ways to expand the scope and reach of each clinic and to serve more people in the community. The partnership between the community, the partnering institution and DOFA is constantly reviewed to improve the efficiency of the clinics in serving the community and upholding the vision of DOFA to improve access to care.

The clinics are each referred to as a Mission and all Missions so far established are listed below. Some of their activities are pictorially depicted in the next few pages. The pictures feature a variety of activities including direct patient care, oral screening sessions, oral health education sessions at out-patient clinics, maternity clinics, schools, community meetings and sometimes, marketplaces.

<u>Mission I: Idikan Community Dental Clinic, Idikan, Ibadan, Oyo State, Nigeria.</u>

The clinic is in the heart of Idikan, Ibadan, Oyo State Nigeria. The partnering institution is the Department of Community Dentistry of the University of Ibadan Dental School, Ibadan, Nigeria. It was initially established in 1987 by Professor Oke and Dr. Fatunde and adopted as a DOFA clinic in 2008. This clinic has served as a model for subsequent DOFA clinics. The staff at this clinic and the faculty of its partnering institution have served as resource for new clinics that are just getting off the ground.

*To the left, 1987 - Initial location of Idikan Community Dental Clinic, Idikan, Ibadan, Nigeria. The clinic occupied the room with the window to the left with entrance in the area with white paint. The well in front of the house served as the source of water for the neighborhood. We brought water and sterile instruments to the clinic and took instruments back to the dental school for sterilization.*

*2006- New location of the Idikan Community Dental Clinic (ground floor). The upper-level houses Adult Medical Clinic and the Infant Welfare Clinic in Idikan, Ibadan, Oyo State. Nigeria. The building serves as a Primary Health Care Center.*

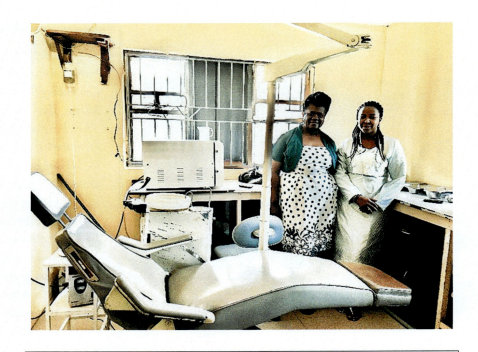

Professor Gbemi Oke (right) and Dr. Adejoke Fatunde
(left) at Idikan Community Dental Clinic, Ibadan, Ibadan
Central Local Government Area, Oyo State, Nigeria

A Dental Outreach event by the University of Ibadan Community
Dentistry team to pregnant women attending prenatal clinic
at Olu Agbebi Maternity Center, Ibadan, Nigeria.

*Dr. Fatunde (2ⁿᵈ from left) with Staff at Olu Agbebi Maternity Center interacting with the pregnant women attending prenatal clinic after the dental outreach.*

*Dr. Fatunde (6ᵗʰ from left), Dr. Taiwo (4ᵗʰ from left) who was the Head of Department in 2013, with Faculty & Residents from the Community Dentistry Department of the University of Ibadan Dental School pose for picture with the Staff of Olu Agbebi Maternity Center after the Oral Health Outreach session.*

Mission II: Ibarapa Community Dental Clinic, Igbo-Ora, Oyo State, Nigeria.

The clinic occupies one of the buildings on the grounds of the Ibarapa Project which is the outreach of the Department of Preventive and Social Medicine of the University of Ibadan Medical School. It is located in Igbo-Ora, Ibarapa East Local Government, Oyo State, Nigeria. The Faculty and Staff of the Department of Community Dentistry of the University of Ibadan Dental School, Ibadan, Nigeria serve as the partnering institution. It was established in 2008.

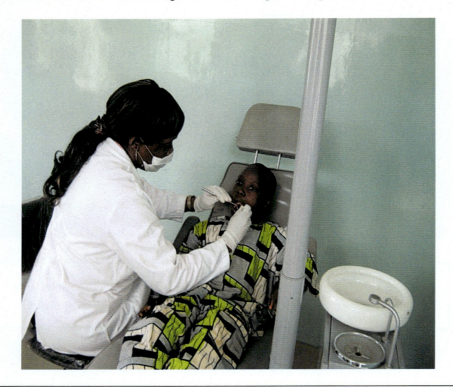

*Dental student (in white coat) performing oral examination on a patient at Ibarapa Community Dental Clinic while on rotation for rural experience.*

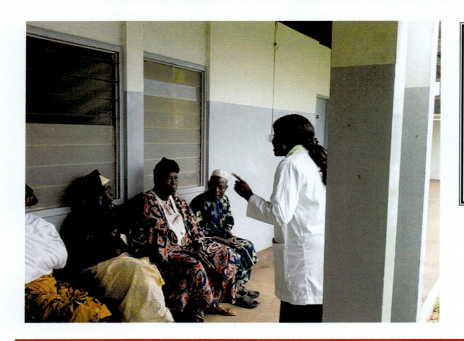

*Dental student (in white coat) providing oral health education to patients awaiting medical treatment at the Igbo -Ora project - located on the same grounds as the Ibarapa Community Dental Clinic in Igbo Ora, Oyo State, Nigeria.*

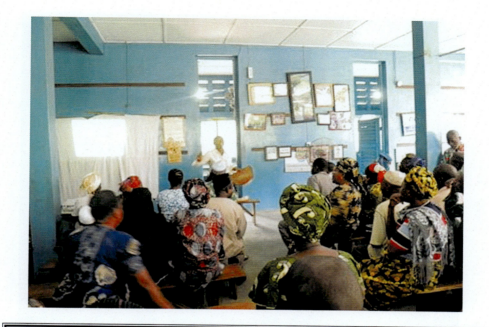

*Community Outreach by the Ibarapa Community Dental Clinic in Igbo-Ora to Awojobi Hospital in Eruwa. Both are located in Ibarapa East Local Government, Oyo State of Nigeria. Picture shows one of the Community Dentistry Residents giving instructions on oral health care at the outpatient clinic.*

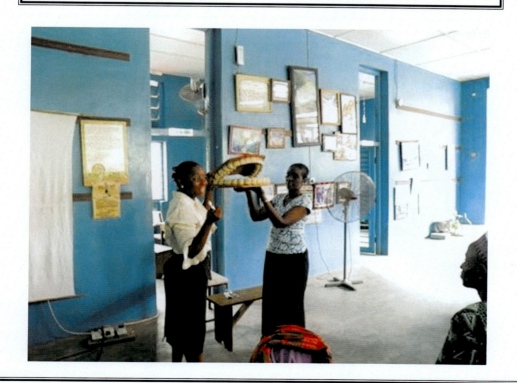

*Dental Residents from University of Ibadan Dental School demonstrating oral health practices on a model to the patients attending out-patient clinic at Awojobi Hospital, Eruwa which is 3km away from the Ibarapa Community Dental Clinic in Igbo-Ora, Oyo State, Nigeria.*

*Dr. Fatunde (1ˢᵗ from right), on behalf of DOFA addressing patients in the outpatient clinic at Awojobi Hospital, Eruwa. Dr. Taiwo, Head of Community Dentistry at the University of Ibadan Dental School (2ⁿᵈ from right), standing by.*

*Dental Outreach to Medical Outpatient at Awojobi Hospital, Eruwa. Dr. Fatunde (3ʳᵈ from left) sitting with some of the students and residents of the University of Ibadan Dental School serving at Ibarapa Community Dental Clinic, Igbo-Ora, Oyo State, Nigeria.*

20011- Community Outreach: Community Oral Health Worker demonstrating brushing techniques to students in Igbo-Ora School using a wooden tooth model and toothbrush.

2017- Dr. Fatunde (right) with UCH Staff working at the Ibarapa Community Dental Clinic, Igbo-Ora, Ibarapa East Local Government in Oyo State, Nigeria during a brainstorming session on expanding the scope of service to the community.

<u>Mission III: Pakoto Community, Dental Clinic, Pakoto, Ogun State, Nigeria.</u>

The clinic is located at the site of the outreach center of the Lagos University Teaching Hospital (LUTH) and the University of Lagos Medical School. It is in Pakoto, Ifo Local Government in Ogun State, Nigeria. It was established in 2010. The partnering institution is the Department of Community Dentistry at LUTH and the University of Lagos School of Dentistry, Idi Araba, Surulere, Lagos, Nigeria.

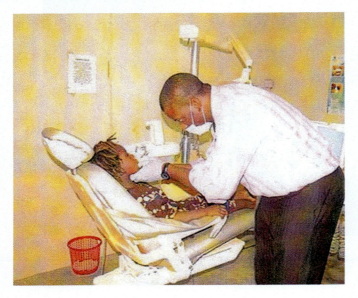

*2010- Oral examination of the first patient seen at the Pakoto Community Dental Clinic by a Resident from LUTH's Dept of Community Dentistry.*

*2010 - First patient (center) treated at Pakoto Community Dental Clinic on inauguration day with Dr. Ogunlewe (left), & Dr. Fatunde (right).*

2009- Inauguration of the Pakoto Community Dental Clinic. The Dental Team for Pakoto Community Dental Clinic. Front from left: Mrs Afolabi-Administrator, Drs Sofola & Uti- Residents in Community Dentistry at LUTH, Dr. Ogunlewe- CMAC LUTH, Dr. Fatunde -DOFA Rep, Dr. Onajole-Director of Pakoto Primary Health Care Center (PHCC) & Head, LUTH Preventive Medicine Dept., Dr. Fawole, Resident. Back Row- Residents & Dental Nurses & Staff.

Dr. Onajole (1st from right), Director of Pakoto PHCC & Head, LUTH Preventive Medicine Department addressing the staff on the inaugural day of the clinic. His message was to inform their friends and family of the availability of dental care at Pakoto PHCC.

*2010 - Dr. Fatunde (1ˢᵗ from left) answering questions from Community Leaders who came to welcome Dental Services to Pakoto PHCC. Each leader got an oral examination and follow up appointment.*

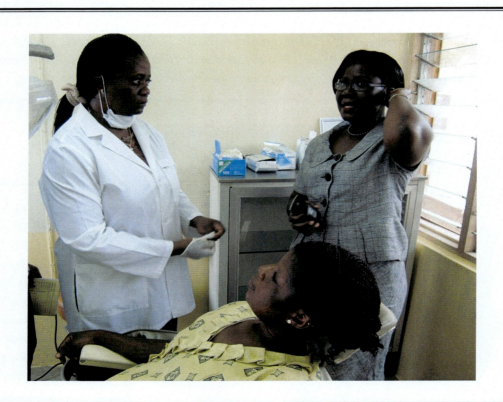

*Dr. Fatunde (left) conferring with Dr. Ogunlewe (right) following examination of patient (center) with a dental abscess at Pakoto Community Dental Clinic.*

2019- With Staff of LUTH and Professor Gbenga Ogunlewe (second from right), Dr, Adejoke Fatunde (third from left) at the Pakoto Community Dental Clinic, Pakoto, Ifo Local Government, Ogun State, Nigeria.

## Mission IV: Kishi Community Dental Clinic, Kishi, Oyo State.

The clinic is located at Kishi Primary Health Care Center, in Kishi, Oyo State. It was initiated in 2014. Credit goes to Mr. Musa Badejoko, an indigene of Kishi who traveled about five hours to seek eye care at Awojobi Hospital in Eruwa, three kilometers from the Ibarapa Community Dental Clinic. On that very day, the outreach team from the University of Ibadan Dental School and the Ibarapa Community Dental Clinic (Mission II) was invited by the late Dr. Ayodele Awojobi, Proprietor of Awojobi Hospital to give oral health education to patients attending its out-patient clinic.

Having listened to the oral health education session during the outreach event, Mr. Badejoko requested that his community in Kishi needed a community dental center so that the people would not need to travel far for dental care as he traveled for eye care. He mobilized community efforts, visiting the University College Hospital Dental Center in Ibadan many times to advocate for the establishment of the dental clinic.

The Department of Community Dentistry at the University of Ibadan Dental School partnered with DOFA to establish the clinic and took it under its wings, initially sending its residents there to provide service. However, it relinquished its services due to political factors. The Kishi Community was trying to hire a dentist to continue to provide service at the clinic. Unfortunately, I have not been able to obtain an update.

Pictures of the clinic are unavailable but below is Mr. Musa Badejoko whose relentless efforts led to the establishment of the clinic.

*Mr. Musa Badejoko, a Kishi indigene who advocated for the establishment of Kishi Community Dental Clinic.*

Mission V: Eni-Osa Community Dental Clinic, Eni-Osa, Ibadan, Oyo State, Nigeria

This is one of the newer clinics adopted by DOFA in 2019. It is located at the Eni-Osa Primary Health Care Center in Eni-Osa, in Ibadan outskirts, Oyo State, Nigeria. The partnering institution is the Department of Community Dentistry of the University of Ibadan Dental School, Ibadan, Nigeria.

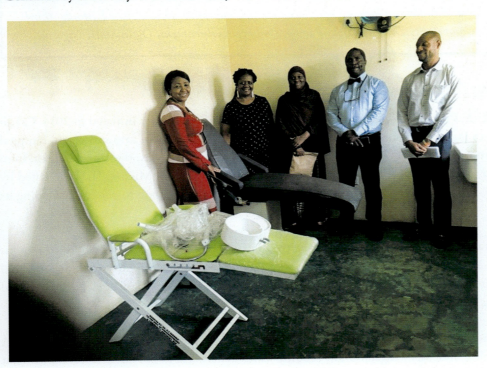

*2019 - Setting up Eni-Osa Clinic: From left to right: Professor Oke, Dr. Fatunde, Dr. Lawal, Dr. Ibiyemi and a Resident from the Community Dentistry Department of the University of Ibadan Dental School, Ibadan, Nigeria.*

*2019- With the team for Eni- Osa Community Dental Clinic from Left to Right: Professor Oke, Dr. Lawal, Nursing Matron for Eni-Osa Primary Health Care Center. Next is Dr. Ibiyemi, the Head of Department, flanked by two Residents, all from the Community Dentistry Department at University of Ibadan Dental School. Dr. Fatunde is at the extreme right.*

Mission VI: Ile-Oluji Community Dental Clinic, Ile-Oluji, Ondo State, Nigeria

This clinic is located at the Oke Alafia Primary Health Care Center in Ile-Oluji, Ondo State, Nigeria. The partnering Institution is the Department of Community Dentistry at the University of Medical Sciences (UNIMED) in Ondo, Ondo State, Nigeria. The site visit was completed in March 2019 by DOFA and the building that houses the clinic was completed by the community in December 2019 under the leadership of the Jegun Olu-Ekun, Oba Olufaderin Adetimehin, the paramount ruler of Ile-Oluji.

*2019- At the site visit to initiate the Ile-Oluji Community Dental Clinic: Left to Right: Dr. Osuh\*, Dr Ibiyemi\*, Professor Oke\*, Oba Olufaderin Adetimehin, Kabiyesi (the Ruler) of Ile-Oluji flanked by his chiefs and Dr. Fatunde, DOFA representative (4ᵗʰ from right). Dr. Lawal\* in green and a Resident\* are to the extreme right. (\*-Staff of the University of Ibadan Community Dentistry Department).*

Following this, DOFA supplied equipment, instruments, and supplies. Although operations were delayed by Covid-19, the formal launching of the clinic was part of the 2022 World Oral Health Day celebrations by UNIMED in March 2022. To date, over fifty patients have been treated at the clinic. Continuity of service in the future is sustainable with the faculty, staff and students of the Community Dentistry Department of UNIMED serving as providers. This clinic is a tri-apatite partnership between DOFA, UNIMED and the Ile-Oluji community.

*Ile Oluji Community Dental Clinic, located at the Oke Alafia Primary Health Care Center in Ile-Oluji, Ondo State Nigeria. Official commissioning of the clinic occurred in March 2022 as part of the 2022 World Oral Health Day activities organized by UNIMED.*

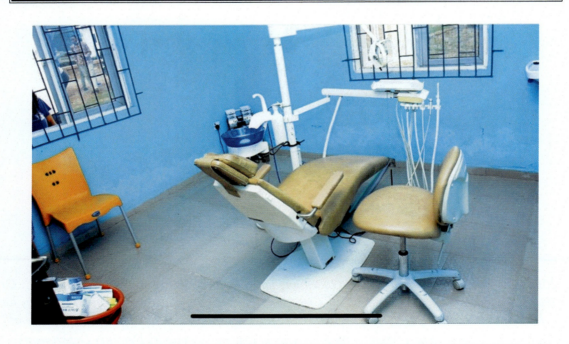

*Inside view of the Ile-Oluji Community Dental Clinic in Ile-Iluji, Ondo, State, Nigeria.*

The Jegun Olu-Ekun and Paramount Ruler of Ile-Oluji, Oba Olufadering Oluwole Adetimehin led the community in completing the building that houses the Ile-Oluji Community Dental Clinic. Here he is commissioning the clinic for service to the community in March 2022 while his chiefs and members of the community look on.

Members of the Ile-Oluji community with faculty, staff and students from the University of Medical Sciences (UNIMED) most of whom are in white coats at the commissioning of the Ile-Oluji Community Dental Clinic in Ile-Oluji, Ondo State, Nigeria in March 2022. UNIMED's Faculty of Dentistry oversees operations at the clinic while its staff, residents, fellows and upper-class students serve as providers.

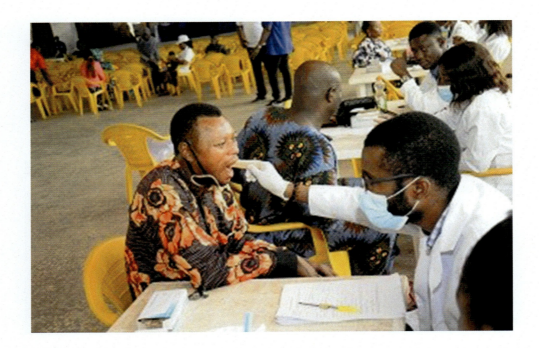

These two pictures show Residents from the Community Dentistry Department at UNIMED performing Oral Screening on attendees at a Town Hall meeting in Ile-Oluji, Ondo State, Nigeria. This was preceded by Oral Health Education session for the Community during the 2022 World Oral Health Day by UNIMED. The attendees were then referred to the Ile-Oluji Community Dental Clinic for primary dental care or to secondary and tertiary dental institutions such as the UNIMED Dental School for additional or advanced care.

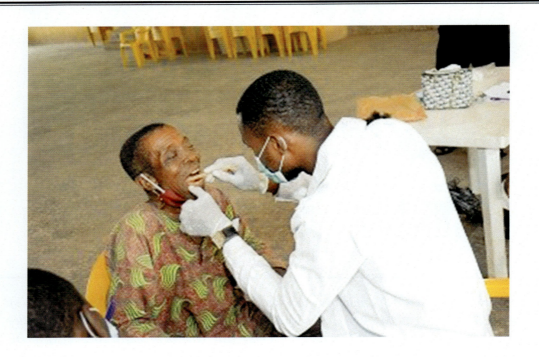

# Beyond the University of Ibadan Dental School
## Section 4: 2010-2020

The fourth decade of my professional life can be described a tripod featuring orthodontic practice, dental outreach, and academia.

## I. Orthodontic Practice

First, I continued to enjoy the practice of orthodontics and have done so in different settings. I slowly eased out of private practice about one third of the way into the fourth decade to enjoy other opportunities which took me to various parts of the United States where, but for work, I might never have visited.

With Familia Dental, my six offices were in six different cities, Clovis, Roswell, Hobbs, Carlsbad, Espanola and Las Cruces, all in New Mexico State. The closest two offices were about two hours apart by car. Working in all six offices was certainly an adventure of a lifetime. I got to travel in New Mexico and appreciate the expanse of land and oil fields in this area. The diversity in the terrain is simply amazing, just as the vegetation. There are the mountains and flat hills that provide a surreal beauty to behold and in contrast, there are plains that cut across New Mexico cities as well. Each office had its own set of assistants and unique team dynamics.

Working with Kool Smiles, I was assigned to El Paso, TX. which is located in the westernmost part of the state of Texas. It lies in the Chihuahuan Desert, nestled between the Franklin Mountains and the Rio Grande Valley. It is a thirty-minute ride across the Bridge of the Americas from Juarez, Mexico. El Paso shares more attributes with New Mexico cities than other Texas cities. It is the only Texas city that falls in the mountain time zone like New Mexico cities while the other Texas cities operate a central time schedule. This was my first visit to west Texas. There, I served as the Orthodontist in five offices but, this time, all five were in the same city in a multi-location corporate setting. Although I had the same team of assistants moving with me from office to office, team coordination was still the key to operating in multiple offices.

In contrast with the desert-like environment in west Texas, my next stop, the city of Corpus Christi where I worked for three years is on the Gulf of Mexico, sheltered by the Padre and Mustang islands. It hosts beaches and bodies of water for miles and miles. The divergence in culture, patient perspectives and availability of dental care between the east and west Texas cities is noticeable and could be significant when compared with the Dallas-Fort Worth Metroplex where I live. There, I worked with Smile Life Orthodontics in just one location, with a constant team of orthodontic assistants, staff, and excellent professional colleagues. It has been an experience to cherish.

I have been privileged to work with great teams at different locations providing care to orthodontic patients. With each team, I have been enriched by the diversity in personalities of members and have learned the value of accommodation in human interactions. Just as members of the body perform distinct functions, each team member brought his or her contributions that impacted the team's outcome and efficiency. We not only worked together to give our patients the best care possible, but we also shared memorable times caring for one another. At the different practices, each team member added his or her uniqueness to the large human quilt that holds meaningful memories for me.

*Dr. Fatunde at Familia Dental, Carlsbad, NM.*

*Dr. Fatunde (1st from left on the back row) with the Orthodontic team at Kool Smiles, El Paso, TX. The team was celebrating a member's birthday.*

*Dr. Fatunde (2nd from left on the front row) with Dr. Cami Martin, also in white coat and the Orthodontic team at Smile Life Orthodontics, Corpus Christi, TX.*

Dr. Fatunde at Smile Life Orthodontics, Corpus Christi, TX.

## II: Dental Missions

Secondly, I continued to take part in dental missions in the USA, volunteering at the triage stations with Mission of Mercy in Texas (TMOM) and New Mexico (NMOM). Periodically throughout the year, Mission of Mercy events are held to offer pro-bono dental services to the uninsured and the underserved. These experiences give me continuous exposure to the need of the dentally underserved.

Dr. Fatunde volunteering at Texas Mission of Mercy (TMOM) event. Note in the background, treating stations where dental care is provided to patients by volunteer dental professionals.

*Dr. Fatunde (2nd from left) with fellow volunteers at a New Mexico Mission of Mercy (NMMOM) event.*

My mission with DOFA also continued to grow. In 2017, DOFA celebrated thirty years of service at the Idikan Community Dental Clinic. This event was chaired by the late Professor H.A. Ajagbe who was one of the pioneer teachers at the University of Ibadan Dental School, He had been rightly dubbed the 'Father of Dentistry' within the University Community. It was very touching to hear him say that he was a proud father with his first three children in the dental profession present at the celebration. These were members of the first three sets of students to graduate from University of Ibadan Dental School: The Dean of Dentistry, Professor Wole Dosumu from the third set (Class of 1982), Professor Gbemisola Oke, from the second set (Class of 1981) and myself from the first set (Class of 1980). He also said that he was happy that these children were present in both sexes, male and female and that made him feel fulfilled. Little did I know that was the last time I would see or hear him speak. He passed away the following year.

*2017- Cutting the cake to celebrate 30yrs of service with members of Idikan Community and staff, Community Dentistry Department of the University of Ibadan Dental School. From left to right, Dr. Ibiyemi, Consultant in Community Dentistry, Professor Denloye, Sub Dean Dentistry, Idikan Community leader, Professor H.A. Ajagbe (Professor Emeritus in Dentistry and Chairman of the occasion), Professor Oke Initiator & Co-founder of Idikan Community Dental Clinic, Dr. Fatunde, DOFA Executive, Professor Taiwo, (Consultant), House Officer and Dental Nurse at the Idikan Community Dental Clinic, One of the Registrars in Community Dentistry & Dr. Lawal (Senior Registrar, Community Dentistry) at the extreme right.*

*2017- Dr. Fatunde (1st from left) addressing the audience at the celebration of 30yrs of service of the Idikan Community Dental Clinic, Idikan, Ibadan, Oyo-State, Nigeria to the community.*

The year 2020 marks ten years of service at both the Ibarapa Community Clinic in Igbo-Ora, Ibarapa East Local Government, Oyo State and the Pakoto Community Clinic located in Ota Local Government area in Ogun State of Nigeria. These are in partnership with the University of Ibadan Dental School, Ibadan, and the University of Lagos School of Dentistry / Lagos University Teaching Hospital in Lagos, respectively. These will also be celebrated after Covid-19 pandemic abates.

## III. Academia

Thirdly, during this decade, I reconnected with academia. I had a brief encounter with teaching, serving as a Consultant to the Boston University Institute for Dental Research and Education (BUIDRE) in Dubai as it tried to graduate its first set of residents in the orthodontic program. BUIDRE, thereafter became the Hamdan Bin Mohammed College of Dental Medicine in Dubai, United Arab Emirates (UAE). This reminded me of my teaching opportunities during the first decade and awakened a willingness to re-engage with academics in orthodontics if the opportunity presents itself.

I also went back to school. I was able to start and complete a doctoral program in an emerging field. In my earlier educational pursuits, I was usually one of the youngest in the class. This time, I was the oldest in my class of eleven. I am blessed with a wonderful family that tolerates my restlessness and brain waves. My husband and children never get tired of drawing out of me, what I do not believe I have that they see. They will work on me until I either see it or start doing what I need to do. I was challenged by the youngest of my four children to think of other things I would want to do in later years. When I mentioned that I would want to teach, she encouraged me to work on getting a doctoral degree. We actually went school shopping together.

In an unplanned series of events, I got admission to the executive Doctoral program in Global Health Systems and Development at Tulane University. My children cheered me on as I traveled to New Orleans, LA, to take twenty hours of classes one weekend a month for twenty-four months. They relentlessly monitored and encouraged me to complete the new doctoral program. I tried to figure out the motivating factor for their super-enthusiasm. Could it be the stories of the unsuccessful attempts at my qualifying examinations and my failure to complete my previous doctoral program that I had shared with them? I had told them about the BDS Part I re-sit examination that I needed to take simply to let them know that sometimes, failure will occur and when it does, you simply get back to the drawing board and try again. They have been witnesses to my failing and retaking dental licensure examinations, watched me cry when I failed and sing when I eventually passed. The qualifying examination is one I failed and gave up on. I wonder if that was the underlying factor behind their determination to get me to finish the new doctoral program.

When I started the program, all my four children were all adults, each pursuing different interests and taking on graduate education. They were on hand at different times to tutor me as needed in statistics, health economics and other subjects that they were better grounded in. Tutorials were sometimes in person and at other times across the ocean by skype and I learnt to work around my tutors' schedules. Quite a reversal of roles it was, but for all of us, it was a memorable adventure for my children to send mom to school and make sure she got through and graduated. For me, failing was just not an option this time, no matter the difficulties I had to endure. I had four beautiful sets of eyes monitoring me and to whom I will always be accountable. I dutifully reported my grades to them each semester and counted it a blessing to receive their adulation when I got good grades or reprimand when I fell short of expectation.

Were they all excited when I passed the qualifying examination, the equivalent of the one I failed that stalled my previous doctoral program? From then on, it was a push to complete the program. They set the deadline. The youngest told me 'Just finish this before you turn sixty'. My husband was very supportive, quietly cheering me to the finish line. A few weeks before my 60th birthday, I defended my dissertation for the Doctor of Science degree (Sc.D.) in Global Health Systems and Development at Tulane University School of Public Health in New Orleans, Louisiana. The eldest of them traveled down to Louisiana for my dissertation defense.

I was very thrilled to have a joint graduation with one of my children who graduated with a master's degree within a week of my graduation in May 2019. Completing the Sc.D. program, I owe to my children who have been my inspiration and motivation. It has certainly given me personal fulfillment.

My practicum experience for the doctoral program featured the effects of maternal stress on the cleft experience of the child. Louisiana State experienced Hurricane Katrina and Hurricane Rita in 2005. Analyzing the birth data from 2005-2008 was highly informative. The stress due to hurricane served as a proxy for other forms of stress a pregnant woman may experience. My doctoral dissertation expanded the concept to include low birth weight in addition to oral cleft, both of which may occur in cleft cases. The message is to minimize the stress in pregnancy to possibly reduce the incidence of oral cleft. Applications of these, I am proposing to evaluate on select populations.

*From left to right, Dr. Ayodeji Fatunde (my husband), Olumadebo Fatunde (son) also graduating and myself.*

*The two 2019 graduands in our family: My son, Olumadebo Fatunde (left) and myself (right).*

*Graduating Sc.D. Global Health Systems & Development from*
*Tulane University School of Public Health, New Orleans, LA.*

*With my daughter, Oluwatomilade (left), my husband, Dr. Ayodeji Fatunde (center) and myself (right) at Tulane University graduation.*

*2019- At Tulane University graduation: Left to right, myself, my husband, Dr. Ayodeji Fatunde and Dr. Lisheng Shi, Chairperson of my Doctoral Committee at Tulane School of Public Health in New Orleans, LA., USA.*

## CHAPTER V:

# RECONNECTING WITH THE UI PIONEER DENTAL CLASS AFTER 40 YEARS SINCE GRADUATION FROM DENTAL SCHOOL

It is almost unimaginable that of a cohort of nineteen, I would be able to reconnect with almost half the class after forty years since I left dental school. Some, I had neither seen nor been in touch with since we graduated in 1980. Yet, as soon as the connection was made in April 2020, the same passion we shared forty to forty-five years ago was re-kindled as the distance of time dissipated. The camaraderie we had in 1975 immediately resurfaced, just as the sense of caring for one another during the five years in dental school.

In the next few pages are photo collages of some of the UI Dental Pioneers, showing what each looked like in 1975 on the left, compared with the ageless and matured faces about forty-five years later to the right. Below each person's photo collage, is a brief description of the remarkable achievements of these notable peers.

I am especially thrilled about their accomplishments and immensely proud of each of them. My gratitude to Dr. Oluwole Ajagbe who initiated the reunion and produced the photo collages. Reconnecting with my dental school peers, even though virtually done, has been one of the highlights of the year 2020. I appreciate each person who has shared his/her achievements with me.

**Joshua A. Folaranmi, BDS, FWACS, FICS, fss, mss, Dss.**

*Col. Joshua Akintoye Folaranmi (Rtd)*
*Col. Folaranmi retired from the Nigerian Army as Chief Consultant in Restorative Dentistry with multiple honors:*
*fss - Forces Service Star, mss- Meritorious Service Star and Dss - Distinguished Service Star.*
*He was an Adjunct Lecturer in Restorative Dentistry at the University of Medical Sciences, (UNIMED), Ondo,*
*Nigeria. He currently runs a multi-location private dental practice in Lagos, Enugu & Port Harcourt, Nigeria.*

**Ademola Olaitan, BDS, FMCDS, FWACS, PNMC.**

*Professor Ademola Abayomi Olaitan*
*Professor Olaitan is Professor of Oral & Maxillofacial Surgery at Lagos State University College of Medicine*
*(LASUCOM) and a Consultant at the Lagos State University Teaching Hospital, both in Lagos, Nigeria.*
*He is the immediate past Dean of Dentistry at LASUCOM.*

**Oluwatosin Sanu, BDS, FWACS, FWFO, MPH.**

*Professor Oluwatosin Oluyemi Sanu* nee Ogunjobi
*Professor Sanu is a Professor of Orthodontics at the Faculty of Dental Sciences and Head of Department of Child Oral Health at College of Medicine of the University of Lagos in Lagos, Nigeria. (CMUL). She is also a Consultant Orthodontist at the Lagos University Teaching Hospital (LUTH), Lagos, Nigeria.*

**Chika, Akamnonu, BDS, DDS.**

*Dr. Chika Agnes Akamnonu,* nee Umeh
*Dr. Akamnonu practiced Dentistry exclusively as a private Dental Practitioner while in Nigeria. She migrated to the USA and obtained her DDS degree and Certificate in General Dentistry from New York University College of Dentistry (NYUCD) in New York City, NY, USA.*
*In the USA, Dr. Akamnonu has worked in diverse dental settings and is settled in Massachusetts, USA. Presently, she works as General Practice Dentist and Dental Attending, supervising Advanced Education in General Dentistry (AEGD) Residents in Western Massachusetts. She is an active member of the American Dental Association.*

**Adetayo Banjo, BDS, MBA.**

*Dr. Adetayo Banjo*
*Following graduation from Dental School, Dr. Banjo, spent his Housemanship or internship year at the University of Ife Teaching Hospital (UNIFE) in Ile Ife, Nigeria. After his National Youth Service at Specialist Hospital in Benin City, Nigeria, he returned to UNIFE as teaching staff in Dental Anatomy. Dr. Banjo felt the pull towards business and left UNIFE as a Registrar to undertake an MBA degree in Chicago, Illinois, USA. He is an Entrepreneur and Philanthropist.*

**Oluwole Ajagbe, BDS, MS.**

*Dr. Oluwole Albert Ajagbe*
*For his postgraduate education, Dr. Ajagbe studied Oral Pathology at Georgetown University, Washington DC., USA. Thereafter, he served on the Faculty the Oral Pathology Department of Howard University Dental School, also in Washington, DC, USA. He is recipient of many awards in clinical dentistry and research. Currently, he is a practicing dentist, running On-Demand Tele Dentistry & Concierge Dental Sleep Medicine.*

Celestine Mbakogu, BDS.

**Dr. Ifeanyi Celestine Mbakogu**

Dr. Mbakogu served at the Military Hospital & The Army School of Medical Sciences in Nigeria. He has been in private practice for over 30years as the Medical Director & Proprietor of Cimbak Dental Clinic, in Port Harcourt, Nigeria. He practices different aspects of dentistry and is a member of the American Academy of Implant Dentistry.

Itam Eigbe, BDS, MSc. (Lon), DDPH, RCS (Eng.), PG Dip (Canada)

**Dr. Itam Eigbe,** *nee Okon*

Dr. Eigbe has had a rich experience practicing dentistry in many countries and within different cultures across Nigeria, England, Netherlands and Canada. She has extensive training in Dental Public Health.

While in Nigeria, she served on the Faculty of the University of Lagos Dental School in Idi-Araba, Lagos. She was also the Managing Director of Livingsprings Dental Clinic in Warri, Nigeria. She has now hung up her drill and is retired comfortably in Canada where she resides with her husband.

**Osagie Akpata, BDS, FWACS, FICD.**

*Professor Osagie Akpata*

*Professor Akpata is a Professor of Oral & Maxillofacial Surgery at the University of Benin (UNIBEN), Benin City, Nigeria. He served as Dean of Dentistry many years ago and recently led the school through the Covid-19 pandemic. He is past President of the Nigerian Association of Oral & Maxillofacial Surgeons. Always a man of faith, Professor Akpata was Chapter President of the Full Gospel Businessmen Fellowship and now serves as Senior Pastor at the Church of God Mission International in Benin City, Nigeria.*

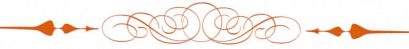

# CHAPTER VI:

# GRATITUDE

The list below is by no means exhaustive, only representative of the men and women without whose efforts I could not have initiated, let alone experience a forty-year dental career.

## College of Medicine, University of Ibadan, Ibadan, Nigeria

- Professor Oluwole Akande, Provost College of Medicine
- Lecturers in the Department of Anatomy, Physiology, Biochemistry, Pathology, Pharmacology, Medicine, Pediatrics, Surgery and Preventive Medicine.

## Department of Dentistry, College of Medicine, University of Ibadan, Nigeria Full Time Faculty:

- Prof Jacob O. Daramola
- Prof Henry A. Ajagbe (RIP)
- Dr. Moronke Noah
- Dr. S.P Luthra (RIP)
- Dr. Kulasekara (RIP)
- Dr. J.O. Lawoyin (RIP)

- Dr. D.O. Lawoyin
- Dr. Bode Falomo
- Dr. Chedha
- Dr. Lanre Bello
- Dr. Dickson Ufomata
- Dr. Dapo Abiose

## Adjunct/Visiting Lecturers/External Examiners:

- Dr. Ajayi-Obe (RIP)
- Dr. Olaniyan (RIP)
- Dr. Aremu
- Dr. Adewunmi
- Prof. Yemi Mosadomi
- Prof. Akpata
- Prof. Akinosi

## Dental Nursing/Hygiene/ Laboratory

- Matron Aluko
- Ms. Titi Odeyemi
- Mr. Tola Oso (RIP)
- Ms. Tope Alonge
- Mrs. Sodeinde
- Mr. Fasan (RIP)
- Mr. Idowu
- Mr. & Mrs. Oluwajana

## University College Hospital, Ibadan, Nigeria

Prof. Taiye Kolawole, Chief Medical Director (RIP)
Mrs. Pat Shenjobi, Director of Administration (RIP)

**University of Michigan, Ann Arbor, MI., USA.**

- o   Dr. Bob Moyers (RIP)
- o   Dr. Peter S. Vig
- o   Dr. Surrender Nanda (RIP)
- o   All Orthodontic Instructors
- o   Dr. Jim McNamara
- o   Ms. Delores Ramsey
- o   Ms. Debbie Stambaugh (RIP)
- o   Ms. Joyce Gunnell (RIP)

**Others**

- ➤   Dr. Adeniran
- ➤   Prof. Frank Okoisor
- ➤   Prof. J. O. Adenubi (*Died before publication*)
- ➤   Dr. Adetola Roberts (RIP)
- ➤   Dr. Elgin Wells
- ➤   Dr. Wayne Joseph
- ➤   Prof. Gbemisola Oke
- ➤   Prof. Olugbemiga Ogunlewe

CHAPTER VII:

# WORDS FROM THE POTTERS

Along my journey in the dental profession, there have been many, whose enthusiasm in the field of dentistry infected me. They willingly shared their skills, knowledge, and expertise, providing me with guidance and constructive feedback. Many had positive attitudes and have been role models to me. Some took personal interest in me and established a mentoring relationship. I have been motivated by the good example they set and watched them meet their professional and personal goals. They value ongoing learning and growth in the field and are respected by colleagues while they listen to and consider the opinions and initiatives of others.

Just as the potter molds the clay and produces different pieces of art, my professional life has been molded by these exemplary men and women. They lifted me up the ladder and continue to hold my hands by their words ringing in my ears, reminding me of lessons to learn, caution to take and clarity needed in my decisions.

Many have moved on to the life beyond. I thank God for bringing them across my path and pray for their sweet repose. Some are still alive, and I proudly share them with you on the following pages.

**Professor J. O. Adenubi**

Dr. Adejoke Fatunde (nee Atanda) was an outstanding student in her graduating class from the University of Ibadan Dental School, Ibadan, Nigeria in 1980.

She reported at our dental school, the University of Lagos School of Dentistry in Lagos, Nigeria for her National Youth Service Corp. She was in our department, the Department of Child Dental Health where she interacted tremendously with her colleagues, teachers and me who at that time, was the Head of Department (HOD).

Early in her career, she showed so much enthusiasm as a young dentist who is well motivated for the career ahead. She was extremely passionate about the dental profession and part of the team that moved the headquarters of the Nigerian Dental Association from Lagos where it had always been since its inception in 1967 to Ibadan in 1980 when she had just become a new dentist. Her passionate address to move the headquarters of the association earned her the name 'Fire brand of Ibadan' from me, the name I still call her whenever I see her.

She was always keen to take on new challenges and we were extremely impressed by her particular interest in orthodontics. So, gladly, we recommended her for postgraduate studies at the University of Michigan, Ann Arbor, Michigan, USA, where she distinguished herself. We are happy that she continues to be outstanding in her specialty.

Over the years, learning of her performance as a clinician, teacher and researcher continue to make us proud of her achievements. It is a delight personally, to contribute to her write up about her dental experience over the last forty years. We wish her continued success in the years ahead.

Prof. J.O. Adenubi
Professor emeritus, Department of Child Dental Health
School of Dentistry, University of Lagos, Lagos, Nigeria

*(Professor Adenubi passed away in November 2020 after he had sent in his write up. His contribution to my professional development remains indelible.)*

**Dr. (Mrs.) Olufadekemi O. Adewunmi**

I am delighted to be recognized as one of the 'porters' that contributed professionally into moulding Dr. Mrs. Adejoke Fatunde (nee Atanda). Today, besides being a dentist, she has become a tree in her specialty, Orthodontics and recognized at home here in Nigeria, in the Kingdom of Saudi Arabia and in the United States of America.

I met 'Dejoke in 1977, when I was employed as an Associate Lecturer in Orthodontics at the Dental School of the University of Ibadan, Ibadan, Oyo State, Nigeria. I was in full-time employment with the Oyo State Ministry of Health. I got invited to teach orthodontics, as there was no other orthodontist in Ibadan. Remembering how I found myself in that field, I readily accepted the job, on part-time basis.

She was in the first set of dental students in a class of sixteen – seven females and nine males. Although all the students were thrilled about the outcome of orthodontics, most of the male students were more interested in surgery, disliked and would rather avoid practical orthodontics, if they could! But there were three students who showed keen interest in orthodontics, two females – Adejoke Atanda and Olutosin Ogunjobi (as they were then known) and one male – Oluwole Ajagbe. Today, these two females are Consultant Orthodontists, while Oluwole Ajagbe is an Oral Pathologist.

Initially, I found it difficult to differentiate Adejoke from Olutosin. They looked physically alike and with even large eyeballs. They were very prompt with their practical work and rivalled each other in class assessments and tests. However, Adejoke got closer to me and she thus became our "big daughter". In fact, the only flower girl at her wedding was our youngest child, Ore-Oluwa.

Realizing that these two ladies were very much interested in orthodontics, I deliberately encouraged them by discussing the advantages of this specialty of Dentistry for women and the prospects of rising fast in the field. As at that time, there were only two female orthodontists in Nigeria! They both went ahead to train and specialize in orthodontics, 'Dejoke in the USA and Tosin in Nigeria while Oluwole Ajagbe trained as an Oral Pathologist in the USA.

Personally, I feel elated to see two of the sixteen who stated off as dental students in their set become orthodontists. They both attended the same secondary school as I did, Queen's School, even though, I attended the ede campus while they went to the Ibadan campus years later. I wonder whether the Queen's spirit drove us three to orthodontics?!

Historically, this is a playback of my trail in the field of orthodontics. I was in the first set of dental students in the first Dental School in Nigeria and the sub-saharan Africa, the University of Lagos Dental School. Nine of us started off in September 1966 and completed our training in June 1971. There was no orthodontist on the staff of the Dental School and the College of Medicine, Lagos, had to invite late Dr. 'Sinmi Johnson to be an Associate Lecturer in Orthodontics. Dr. Johnson was in full-time employment with the Ministry of Health, Lagos. She was the first Nigerian Orthodontist who had trained in the United Kingdom. It was this lady's charm, mannerisms and wonderful treatment results which attracted me into this seemingly feminine specialty of dentistry!

I worked closely with Dr. Johnson and my interest in her subject led her to encouraging me to pursue orthodontics for my specialty training. She wasted no time in introducing me to her alma mater, the Glasgow Dental School and Hospital, Glasgow, Scotland. On her recommendation, I received the In-service training fellowship of the then Western State of Nigeria to study orthodontics in that same institution in Scotland between September 1974 and December 1975. This earned me the diploma, D.D. Ortho. of the Royal College of Physicians and Surgeons of Glasgow. Thus, I became the second Orthodontist in Nigeria!

It is fulfilling, personally, that out of the first set of sixteen dental students in the second Dental School in Nigeria, two turned out today to be Fellows in Orthodontics. To God be the glory! Dejoke had always been a brilliant and hardworking, yet very humble. In the motto of our secondary school, Queen's School, I say to you 'Dejoke, 'PASS ON THE TORCH'! I am proud and happy to be part of your success story in Dentistry, particularly in Orthodontics.

Congratulations and keep the flag flying, even higher!!!

---

Dr. Mrs. Olufadekemi O. Adewunmi
B.D.S.(Lagos); D. D. Ortho., RCPS (Glasgow); FWACS; FMCDS.
Retired Chief Consultant Orthodontist.
August 1, 2020.

**Professor J. O. Daramola**

Upon completion of my studies in London and returning to Nigeria in October 1973, it was by providence that, in 1975, I was appointed the first Lecturer and Consultant in Dentistry. I was also made the Head of the Department of Dentistry of the University College Hospital in Ibadan, Nigeria. It was a small department then, but there were visionary plans to expand the department into a full-fledged dental center and an associated School of dentistry.

I was charged with the heavy responsibility of implementing the proposals for establishing a School of Dentistry at the University of Ibadan, Ibadan, Nigeria. The associated University College Hospital was also no longer content with the small dental unit it had under the umbrella of the department of Plastic Surgery. They wanted a Dental Center that catered for all aspects of dentistry to all patients. The proposals, including the curriculum, had been prepared by a team of senior academics from Nigeria and the United Kingdom. The team that was on the ground for execution of the proposals had limited experience but the duty we were given was not negotiable; we had to start the academic and clinical programmes for the dental students.

As could be imagined, at that time, we faced many difficult challenges: recruitment of staff, setting-up of the clinical facilities, including the purchase and storage of the expensive and temperature sensitive dental materials. The electric power and water supply, both essential infrastructures needed in most dental settings, were most unreliable to say the least. Nevertheless, the clinical facilities for the training of an annual intake of fifty had to be up and running within two years. In addition to the responsibilities of training the dental students, I also had to take on the administrative running of the Department of Dentistry and yet, be accountable to the College of Medicine and the University of Ibadan Senate.

As a result of the hard work of colleagues with whom I worked and others who came after us, many of them graduates of University of Ibadan School of Dentistry, the single Department of Dentistry has evolved into a full-fledged Faculty of Dentistry of the University of Ibadan with five departments, namely, Oral and Maxillofacial Surgery, Restorative Dentistry, Child Oral Health, Periodontology and Community Dentistry and Oral Pathology/ Oral Medicine. The Faculty of Dentistry also offers Postgraduate Program culminating in the Master's degree in

Dental Sciences (MDS) degree. Programmes in Dental Public Health leading to both the Master's degree and Diploma are expected to follow soon. I look back with great joy and pride at the accomplishments of University of Ibadan School of Dentistry that I was privileged to initiate.

Looking back through the forty years since our pioneer dental students graduated, I have felt very privileged to have had the opportunity to mould and influence the professional lives of the first graduating class. They studied and trained under difficult conditions. Less than twenty of those who started the dental programme, made it to final year and only a subset of these graduated in 1980 as the first set of dental graduates of the University of Ibadan, Ibadan, Nigeria.

I am immensely proud of their success and professional accomplishments in the various specialties of dentistry in which they have worked, which has been due to continued hard work and unwavering belief in their abilities. I have recently been able to re-establish contact and share professional experiences with many of them and I am thrilled at their accomplishments. I feel personally fulfilled that I was able to contribute to their professional training and development.

I am glad that Adejoke Atanda then, one of the pioneer students, has found it necessary and important to record her personal experience as a pioneer student to inform and educate the younger generations. As a student, Miss Atanda was eager to learn, unafraid to ask questions and had a high sense of commitment to her studies. I was impressed with the way she talked passionately about dentistry. After graduation, Dr. Atanda proceeded to the United States for postgraduate professional training in Orthodontics at the University of Michigan, Ann Arbor and became an Orthodontist. She practices and lives in the United States.

It has been my pleasure to make a written contribution to her memoir and wish her the best in the future.

Jacob O. Daramola, BDS (Lond), LDS RCS (Eng)
FDS RCPS (Glasg), FNMC, FWACS.
Retired Professor of Oral & Maxillofacial Surgery

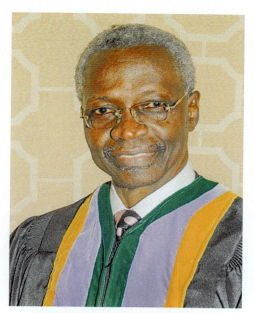

**Professor Davidson Lawoyin**

It gives me a tremendous joy to express few words on Dr. Adejoke "Ayinke" Fatunde who by the special grace of God I have known for over fifty years thereabout. Long before my interaction with her at the professional and social level, her lovely late parents have been known to me. Whatever she is today, is by the Grace of God and the intensely caring parents that brought her forth.

Our path crossed formally and professionally in the year !1978 when myself and my late twin brother (Professor Jonathan Lawoyin) returned to Nigeria to join the faculty of the College of Dentistry, University of Ibadan. Dr. Fatunde being a member of the foundation class at that time easily became noticeable even though we have parted ways for years. Naturally, I became close to her not only as a teacher but as a brother. One thing that stood out about Dr. Fatunde is her resiliency, doggedness and the "can do" spirit she demonstrated at all times. Where she derives her strength to engage her rigorous daily routines will continue to amaze me. I call her "Ayinke" which is her pet name (oriki) out of shear endearment. She is focused like a laser, well organized and she coupled this with a deep sense of self awareness.

The day she told me that she would like to pursue Orthodontics as her sub-specialty, my jaw dropped simply because I know that the curriculum in orthodontics have not been fully developed and integrated at that point in the dental school. Nothing will deter this woman with a steely resolve, for after all. where there is a will there is a way. She will later be sponsored by the College to Ann Arbor Michigan to pursue her postgraduate studies in orthodontics.

The rest is history, because today Dr. Adejoke Ayinke Fatunde is a board- certified orthodontist in the State of Texas. Her unyielding persuasiveness for academic and clinical excellence is legendary. When I look back, I still marvel about how she has managed to balance motherhood and the obviously demanding professional and social responsibilities she faced in the early days of this journey.

For those who now see her at the pinnacle of her profession, I believe a glimpse into her past as being presented will surely attest to the fact that the grace of God alone has seen her through all these gloriously. It has been a privilege for me to have her as a worthy colleague and most importantly as my 'aburo' translated as little sister.

Davidson O. Lawoyin, DDS, FICD
Retired Prof of Oral and Maxillofacial Surgery

**Professor Frank Okoisor**

I remember as if it were yesterday, when a young Miss Atanda from Ibadan attending a student conference in Lagos followed me into my office. She said "I told the students I have some problems and I was advised to follow that man" that was me. She was cultured, courteous and confident. I must have helped with solving her problems and we have been friends since then. even, at that time, I knew she would do very well in the profession.

The last time we met was about 25 years ago in Saudi Arabia.

A lady by birth and education - her father was a professor of history. True to her nature, she chose to specialize in an area of dentistry I consider to be very rewarding in the sense that it puts smiles on the face of their patients. This is orthodontics.

Adejoke, in all her endeavors demonstrates good character and learning. I am proud of her achievements and pleased to be her mentor. We wish you many more fruitful years in the service of the profession and your patients to the Greater Glory of God, Amen.

Congratulations on your attaining a glorious milestone in the profession. May the Good Lord continue to bless you.

Aunty and I send our best wishes, with great love.

Frank Okoisor. BDS, FWACS, FNMC
Professor emeritus, Department of Preventive Dentistry
School of Dentistry, University of Lagos (Unilag)
Lagos, Nigeria

CHAPTER VIII:

# FROM THE SUPERVISORS

In the following pages, you will read from my supervisors. Through collaboration, each, led the team to improve productivity and reach the goal with minimal errors. To be a follower, is often easier than being the leader. Being member of a team led by each of these effective supervisors has been a great learning experience that I cherish.

I have learnt from their creativity, communication and mediation skills, organization and versatility. Each is knowledgeable in the field, served as a good coach and negotiator while taking the needs of others into consideration, but remaining goal and result oriented.

**Dr. Camaron Martin**

My name is Dr. Camaron Martin, I am the owner of SmileLife Orthodontics and have practiced in our Corpus Christi location with Dr. Fatunde for the last two years.

Our Corpus Christi office is a large practice starting approximately 800 cases per year. When I decided to bring on an additional doctor, I thought it would take time to find that special person. Someone that had experience, someone with similar philosophies in patient care, someone who would appreciate our staff and continue with their education of not just how to do a procedure, but why. Most importantly, I was a recent graduate, only three years out of residency. I needed, someone who would not overpower my limited experience, but help me grow. I was prepared to take time to find the right doctor but turns out Dr. Fatunde was my first interview. I knew within 30 minutes of meeting her in person that she was the one. I introduced her to the staff shortly thereafter, they gave the thumbs up and Dr. Fatunde joined the team!

Dr. Fatunde has not been what I hoped to find in a doctor, but so much more. Her genuine personality made me feel instantly comfortable to show and discuss with her a handful of cases that I felt were not in good control. I never felt judged, and her advice has always been right on target. She has been, for me a mentor from whom I learn something every day. When it comes to staff, Dr. Fatunde is always up for a lunch learn when she feels they will benefit. We have been able to work together to develop unified treatment plans for our patients while at the same time continuing to pursue interests such as Invisalign and Carriere appliances.

Additionally, her experience has guided me time and again in clinic protocols from hygiene to Covid-19, as well as issues that arise with practice management and staffing decisions. Having someone with such experience and knowledge to discuss treatment concerns as well as to share the joy of a successful outcome has made all the difference in my job satisfaction.

It is my belief the best leaders are those who recognize their weaknesses and then surround themselves with others who have strengths in those areas. Dr. Fatunde is a woman of many strengths. Smile Life Corpus Christi is thriving with her contributions, patients love her, the team enjoys her company and guidance.

I am honored to stand beside her as a colleague, and even more, so blessed to also call her my friend.

Camaron Martin, BDS, MS.
Owner
Smile Life Orthodontics
Corpus Christi, TX.

**Dr. Andre M. Singleton**

I have managed many doctors in my position, some good some not so good.

I have only managed one amazing doctor which is Dr. Fatunde. Dr. Fatunde is a leader, and director and a master of her ship which would be the clinic and her patients.

When you have the pleasure to have such a person that needs no direction to complete their tasks, takes criticism is a positive way, leads her own team and helps others to see their way without putting them down, your job as a supervisor is relatively sweatless.

Dr. Fatunde's personality is just delightful, bubbly and heart filling. It is a pleasure just to sit down with her and soak in all the knowledge that she has to offer. Sometimes I thought Dr. Fatunde was my supervisor.

Dr. Fatunde's patients respect and appreciate all the wonderful things that she was doing for them. The staff just adore her.

When it came to input, Dr. Fatunde is not shy, Dr. Fatunde speaks her mind and there is no mistake about what her point was. What a leader!

I can just talk all day about this wonderful person, but I need to stop. I hope all the best for her and her progress going forward.

God Bless

Andre M. Singleton, BDS
Regional Director. Kool Smiles.

## CHAPTER IX:

# FRIENDS UNFORGETTABLE

These, whose account, you will read in the next few pages have stood with me through thick and thin and supported me in every venture along my professional journey. They are fellow dentists, well accomplished in their respective specialties. We have shared many events and experiences, joyful and painful together. They are my back props with whom I bounce ideas back and forth. They are also my road stops who caution me when I get a brainwave and I am too eager to fly with it. They will dialogue the pros and cons with me to help me get clarity, refine my proposed plans, and assist me in execution of the plans. They each, have been, my colleague, my friend, my sister, and my companion. Each is a definite treasure to me.

**Professor Olugbemiga Ogunlewe**

Adejoke Ariyike Atanda

Adejoke Ariyike Atanda! This was how I knew her. Our friendship dated back to the mid-sixties at Oke-Ado Baptist Church, Ibadan, Nigeria where both of our families worshipped. Our friendship continued through secondary school and the University. As fate would have it, we both studied Dentistry; she went to the University of Ibadan while I was at the University of Lagos. Apart from being childhood friends, we thus became professional colleagues though in different specialties.

I vividly and fondly remember the good time we had together when Adejoke did her one-year compulsory National Youth Service Corps Scheme at the Lagos University Teaching Hospital, Idi-Araba Lagos, while I was doing my internship. We stayed together in my one-bedroom apartment. During this time, she was carrying Tomilade's pregnancy and we both nurtured it until she went to join Deji in the United States.

Over my fifty years of relationship with Adejoke, I find her to be very loving, truthful, and always willing to help. I admire her capacity and tenacity in successfully combining the management of her professional, marital and family responsibilities. Since the early exit of her mother, she assumed the responsibility of providing leadership for her siblings. Adejoke is a 'mother hen!'. She is extremely hard working at whatever she sets her mind to do and she ensures she achieves it. No wonder, she graduated with a Doctor of Science degree at over 60years.

In the field of dentistry, she had contributed immensely to ensuring that dental services get to the grass root in Nigeria through her Dental Outreach for Africa (DOFA) initiative. As a professional colleague, she encouraged and supported me in setting up a dental clinic at our Primary Health Center in Pakoto, Ogun State, Nigeria, while I served as the Chairman, Medical Advisory Council (CMAC) of the Lagos University Teaching Hospital (LUTH). This falls within the objectives of her DOFA organization. The Chief Medical Director of LUTH then, Professor Akin Osibogun fully embraced the project. The Pakoto Community Dental Clinic serves as a dental outreach for LUTH and has been serving the Community for the last ten years with on-going support from DOFA. Adejoke has left her dental footprints in the sand time!

It is heart-warming to note that marriage and migration has not affected our relationship rather our friendship has metamorphosed into a family relationship and this continues to fester.

The Yorubas have an adage that says 'Ogun omode ki sere gba ogun odun'. This means that twenty children usually do not remain friends for twenty years. Our friendship has defiled this! I am therefore excited to contribute this piece to this memoir.

M. Olugbemiga Ogunlewe, BDS, FWACS, FIAOMS.
Professor, Oral & Maxillofacial Surgery
University of Lagos Faculty of Dental Sciences, Lagos, Nigeria
Consultant Oral Surgeon
Lagos University Teaching Hospital (LUTH), Lagos, Nigeria
Coordinator, LUTH Cleft Team/Smile Train

**Professor Gbemisola Aderemi Oke**

Rarely does any write- up take me this long to compose. But Adejoke Ariyike Fatunde is not the ordinary person by any standard. The multifaceted nature of her life demands volumes, instead of this single autobiographical project. I therefore struggled with combining the books: 'Adejoke of a noble birth, solid faith and love-filled foundation' along with another book on the 'gargantuan responsibility placed on her delicate frame as an adolescent after the tragic loss of her mother and only sister'. Or how could you hope to trace the life of "Dejoke as an Orthodontist, first in academia to one who has served diverse populations across the globe, without devoting a whole book? Then of course, the aspects of her life as oldest sibling, a wife, mother and friend would be a Bestseller. What about Adejoke our own 'Activist' and her Non-Governmental Organization (DOFA), through which she keeps blessing dental schools and populations?

Having said this let me start from when I first met Adejoke Ariyike Fatunde, then Atanda. That was when I became a clinical dental student of dentistry at the University of Ibadan in 1978. Adejoke was my senior because she belonged to the first set at the Dental school, while I was in the second cohort. Students in the two sets were close because we were few and shared experiences unique to pioneers and that formed the foundation of a lifelong friendship. even though she was of a slight frame at the time, one could not help noticing Adejoke because, she was the Class Representative. She, along with a couple of others, founded the Dental Student Association and took up its administration. Through this, Adejoke initiated a series of activism for visibility for the 'relatively unknown' field of dentistry until they shone the spotlight on it.

Later as a young Dentist, she led a massive movement for identity of the profession and this culminated in some memorable achievements; first the inclusion of 'Dental' in 'Nigerian Medical Council' (NMC), thus translating the agency to the' Medical and Dental Council of Nigeria'(MDCN). Like this was the elevation of the status of the Ibadan Dental School, when the long-ranged visionary, Adejoke, moved to shift the Headquarters of the Nigerian Dental Association from its 'traditional' base at Lagos to Ibadan. The strategy that accomplished this feat is enough to fill another chapter.

'Dejoke' has always been one who cultivates lifetime friendship with peers and the older one. I remember that she had a special, cordial relationship with virtually all our seniors in the medical and dental profession, each being referred to as 'Brother Jare, Sister Fade, Brother Bode etc. This was one attribute I admired and emulated to some extent. In the same way, she formed special bonds with other professional and support staff and accorded each their dues; another lesson I learnt from this younger friend of mine. It is Dejoke who taught me how a relationship started on friendship becomes more meaningful and rewarding when upgraded to family status. Adejoke has, in addition to me, friends who by Yoruba parlance are referred to as *'Ore d'ebi'*; meaning, friend who has become family. Consequently, the families of Ayodeji and Adejoke Fatunde along with that of Bankole and Gbemisola Oke are well knitted together.

Dejoke has had a significant impact on my profession and conduct. everyone who has ever encountered her knows how hard working Adejoke is. She has extraordinary capacity for work, and she mobilizes other to follow suit. If there ever was any trace of doggedness attributed to my person, Adejoke would conveniently account for the majority. The story of the Idikan Primary Oral Health Centre, from inception to almost 40 years after cannot be separated from the influence of this friend of mine. When the idea came to me, I had hardly voiced it out when Adejoke gave life to it, supporting the idea with her time, money and technical competences. Till date, Idikan, which has been replicated to other sites, continues to receive support and supplies on a regular basis from DOFA.

I have learnt and continue to enjoy the dividends of true friendship from Dejoke. Always a phone call away, she gives a shout out like you are just next door. She remembers every special moment and has a keepsake to mark each, no matter how small. She is so trusting and dependable thus teaching you also the need to be dependable. Adejoke is a unique person.

I wish her many more useful years and exploits.

Gbemisola Aderemi Oke
BDS, MPH, Ph.D., FMCDS (Nig)
Professor, Community Dentistry
Faculty of Dentistry
University of Ibadan, Ibadan, Nigeria.

## CHAPTER X:

# MY MOTIVATORS AND DESTINY HELPERS

*With my husband, Dr. Ayodeji Fatunde*

My deepest gratitude to my husband who has accommodated my restlessness and often spontaneous decisions. Most of these, I made knowing I had his support and that he would somehow find a way to adjust accordingly and hold up the fabric of the family whether I was home or away. My confidence in him has been the wind beneath my wings that has allowed me to breathe freely, fly whenever I saw the need to and perch when I need to take a break. Freedom to be me, has been the fuel that runs my engine.

My eldest child, Oluwatomilade may never know the width of gratitude in my heart for her. Still a child herself, and during her vulnerable pre-teen and teenage years, she took care of her siblings with such devotion and unending love while mom was studying for an examination or undertaking an exercise in the journey of her dental career. Till today, she remains mother-hen to her siblings, a source of joy to my heart. She is always there to lead and guide.

*With family: left to right - Olumadebo, Olumurejiwa, myself,*
*my husband, Oluwatomilade and Olubadewa at the back.*

Olubadewa always has his head levelled on his neck and his cool demeanor and humor often kept me calm through the rough waters. He has navigated some scenes uncharted by me with such courage and determination that have helped increased my own faith. He has a positive outlook that is often infectious and this, many times has lifted my spirit.

Olumadebo remained in quiet muse most of these years. I sense he might have wondered many a times, when his mother would eventually settle down in one place. One thing is sure, he has his vision and ideas in view even when he does not communicate them clearly to the rest of us. We have all learned to be patient and let his actions speak to us when the time is right. I always feel his compassion and love whether spoken or unspoken.

As for Olumurejiwa, what can I say? I see a little of myself in her and I have a lot of respect for her being a much better version, doing many things I did not have the courage to undertake. Her audaciousness never ceases to amaze me. I have learnt a lot from her tenacity and focus.

I also thank God for Rechel Oby and Jasmine, my two special daughters from whom I have drawn a lot of inspiration.

They all are my blessings, my motivators and destiny helpers. Every waking moment, I thank God for each of them.

*With family: Showcase of our Nigerian heritage, left to right - Oluwatomilade, Rechel Oby, myself, my husband, Olubadewa, Olumurejiwa, Jasmine and Olumadebo*

## Those who will come Beyond: The Next Generation

Olufimidara is the first of the next generation of my progeny. She gives me great hope of what is to come that I may or may not have the privilege to witness in the lives of my future descendants.

*Obiageli Adejoke Olufimidara Ajoke*

It is primarily for her and others to follow that I decided to document my journey over the last forty years in dentistry. Might any of them go into dentistry? Maybe, maybe not.

I pray for favor, guidance, wisdom, and empowerment in whichever field each of my progeny chooses to engage. I pray that they will have more opportunities than I have been privileged to experience. I pray that each of them will be blessed beyond measure and will be for signs and wonders of God in their generation (Isaiah 8:18). Amen.

## CHAPTER XI:

# CONCLUSION

As I reflected at the beginning of 2020, thinking of what I should do during the year, I ended up visiting the past, and was in awe of the goodness of God and His abounding grace through these forty years. Going down memory lane became addictive in depth and frequency, more than my usual private recollections that I have engaged in from time to time. This time, I felt I should document not just in my mind but write in order to share my experience with my generations to come. Reporting my experiences by the decades has allowed me to take an in-depth review of the different stages of my professional life.

I have been blessed to enjoy diversity in professional experiences, many of which fell on my lap. The first decade featured different opportunities to train and practice in my select specialty. In the second decade, the dearth of opportunities that I experienced in its early part was at first unsettling and thrust me to dig into dental public health. At the time, my thought was, if dental licensure was not attainable for me to practice orthodontics, I was going to get engaged in dental public health. The struggle lasted a while but, I was able to get back into clinical orthodontic practice in the second half of the second decade.

What I thought was my alternate plan, dental public health became another path for me to tread. I became encumbered with the need to increase access to dental care to the underserved, a need that is apparently more global in its scope than I ever imagined. This led to my establishing Dental Outreach for Africa, Inc. in later years. The years that appeared to be full of uncertainty eventually led me to into activities that have become part of my professional service. The vision of Dental Outreach for Africa Inc. (DOFA) has become part of my life's mission.

In the third decade, I continued to practice orthodontics in various settings, Corporate offices, Dental Service Organizations, Solo Private Practice and Group Practice. Each came with its own clinical dynamics, patient pool, administrative complexities and professional politics that teaches various aspects of professional and human interaction. I got to travel, and sometimes, I wondered if my restless self would not have been bored without these opportunities. These adventures have given a unique flavor to my professional and personal life.

The fourth decade allowed me to enjoy both orthodontics and dental public health, a combination that is somewhat unusual, but one which I have found very fulfilling. During this fourth decade, I also got a second chance at starting and this time, completing my doctoral degree with the encouragement of my children. Getting the Sc.D. degree is icing on the cake, a delicious cake that I keep biting in small pieces.

Where do I go from here?

I hope to continue the same activities of the fourth decade and pray for more grace, additional years in health and strength to grow in my horizons. In addition, I am open to serving wherever needed, in teaching and consultancy even as I continue with orthodontic practice and other activities in dental public health.

Life and age will bring in many more challenges, I am sure. I thank God for the opportunities that I have had in the last forty years. I am savoring what He has helped me to accomplish so far. If I designed my own life, I could not have produced a better design. I look back and see several things I could have done better, but hindsight is always twenty-twenty. Might I have had a better outcome? Maybe. There is always room for improvement.

I am certain that I could not have conjured the grace and benevolence that sustained me through the last forty years. That, surely, is not my making, but part of the masterplan from my maker. I pray for His leading in the next steps.